Doing Ethnographic and Observational Research

Doing Ethnographic and Observational Research (by Michael Angrosino) is the third part of *The SAGE Qualitative Research Kit*. This *Kit* comprises eight books and taken together the *Kit* represents the most extensive and detailed introduction to the process of doing qualitative research. This book can be used in conjunction with other titles in the *Kit* as part of this overall introduction to qualitative methods but this book can equally well be used on its own as introduction to doing ethnographic and observational research.

Complete list of titles in *The SAGE Qualitative Research Kit*

- Designing Qualitative Research *Uwe Flick*
- Doing Interviews *Steinar Kvale*
- Doing Ethnographic and Observational Research *Michael Angrosino*
- Doing Focus Groups *Rosaline Barbour*
- Using Visual Data in Qualitative Research *Marcus Banks*
- Analysing Qualitative Data *Graham R. Gibbs*
- Doing Conversation, Discourse and Document Analysis *Tim Rapley*
- Managing Quality in Qualitative Research *Uwe Flick*

Members of the Editorial Advisory Board

Doing Ethnographic and Observational Research

Michael Angrosino

Los Angeles | London | New Delhi
Singapore | Washington DC

First published 2007

SAGE Publications Ltd
1 Oliver's Yard
55 City Road
London EC1Y 1SP

SAGE Publications Inc.
2455 Teller Road
Thousand Oaks, California 91320

SAGE Publications India Pvt Ltd
B 1/I 1 Mohan Cooperative Industrial Area
Mathura Road, New Delhi 110 044
India

SAGE Publications Asia-Pacific Pte Ltd
3 Church Street
#10-04 Far Samsung Hub
Singapore 049483

Library of Congress Control Number: 2006938285

British Library Cataloguing in Publication data

A catalogue record for this book is available from the British Library

ISBN 978-0-7619-4975-6

Typeset by C&M Digitals (P) Ltd, Chennai, India
Printed in Great Britain by Ashford Colour Press Ltd.

▋▋ Contents

Editorial introduction
Uwe Flick

- Introduction to *The SAGE Qualitative Research Kit*
- What is qualitative research?
- How do we conduct qualitative research?
- Scope of *The SAGE Qualitative Research Kit*

Introduction to *The SAGE Qualitative Research Kit*

In recent years, qualitative research has enjoyed a period of unprecedented growth and diversification as it has become an established and respected research approach across a variety of disciplines and contexts. An increasing number of students, teachers and practitioners are facing questions and problems of how to do qualitative research – in general and for their specific individual purposes. To answer these questions, and to address such practical problems on a how-to-do level, is the main purpose of *The SAGE Qualitative Research Kit*.

The books in *The SAGE Qualitative Research Kit* collectively address the core issues that arise when we actually do qualitative research. Each book focuses on key methods (e.g. interviews or focus groups) or materials (e.g. visual data or discourse) that are used for studying the social world in qualitative terms. Moreover, the books in the *Kit* have been written with the needs of many different types of reader in mind. As such, the *Kit* and the individual books will be of use to a wide variety of users:

- *Practitioners* of qualitative research in the social sciences, medical research, marketing research, evaluation, organizational, business and management studies, cognitive science, etc., who face the problem of planning and conducting a specific study using qualitative methods.
- *University teachers* and lecturers in these fields using qualitative methods will be expected to use these series as a basis of their teaching.
- *Undergraduate and graduate students* of social sciences, nursing, education, psychology and other fields where qualitative methods are a (main) part of the university training including practical applications (e.g. for writing a thesis).

Each book in *The SAGE Qualitative Research Kit* has been written by a distinguished author with extensive experience in their field and in the practice with methods they write about. When reading the whole series of books from the beginning to the end, you will repeatedly come across some issues which are central to any sort of qualitative research – such as ethics, designing research or assessing quality. However, in each book such issues are addressed from the specific methodological angle of the authors and the approach they describe. Thus you may find different approaches to issues of quality or different suggestions of how to analyze qualitative data in the different books, which will combine to present a comprehensive picture of the field as a whole.

What is qualitative research?

It has become more and more difficult to find a common definition of qualitative research which is accepted by the majority of qualitative research approaches and researchers. Qualitative research is no longer just simply '*not quantitative research*', but has developed an identity (or maybe multiple identities) of its own.

Despite the multiplicity of approaches to qualitative research, some common features of qualitative research can be identified. Qualitative research is intended to approach the world 'out there' (not in specialized research settings such as laboratories) and to understand, describe and sometimes explain social phenomena 'from the inside' in a number of different ways:

- By analyzing experiences of individuals or groups. Experiences can be related to biographical life histories or to (everyday or professional) practices; they may be addressed by analyzing everyday knowledge, accounts and stories.
- By analyzing interactions and communications in the making. This can be based on observing or recording practices of interacting and communicating and analyzing this material.
- By analyzing documents (texts, images, film or music) or similar traces of experiences or interactions.

Common to such approaches is that they seek to unpick how people construct the world around them, what they are doing or what is happening to them in terms that are meaningful and that offer rich insight. Interactions and documents are seen as ways of constituting social processes and artefacts collaboratively (or conflictingly). All of these approaches represent ways of meaning, which can be reconstructed and analyzed with different qualitative methods that allow the researcher to develop (more or less generalizable) models, typologies, theories as ways of describing and explaining social (or psychological) issues.

How do we conduct qualitative research?

Can we identify common ways of doing qualitative research if we take into account that there are different theoretical, epistemological and methodological approaches to qualitative research and that the issues that are studied are very diverse as well? We can at least identify some common features of how qualitative research is done.

- Qualitative researchers are interested in accessing experiences, interactions and documents in their natural context and in a way that gives room to the particularities of them and the materials in which they are studied.
- Qualitative research refrains from setting up a well-defined concept of what is studied and from formulating hypotheses in the beginning in order to test them. Rather, concepts (or hypotheses, if they are used) are developed and refined in the process of research.
- Qualitative research starts from the idea that methods and theories should be appropriate to what is studied. If the existing methods do not fit to a concrete issue or field, they are adapted or new methods or approaches are developed.
- Researchers themselves are an important part of the research process, either in terms of their own personal presence as researchers, or in terms of their experiences in the field and with the reflexivity they bring to the role – as are members of the field under study.
- Qualitative research takes context and cases seriously for understanding an issue under study. A lot of qualitative research is based on case studies or a series of case studies, and often the case (its history and complexity) is an important context for understanding what is studied.
- A major part of qualitative research is based on text and writing – from field notes and transcripts to descriptions and interpretations and finally to the presentation of the findings and of the research as a whole. Therefore, issues of transforming complex social situations (or other materials such as images) into texts – issues of transcribing and writing in general – are major concerns of qualitative research.
- If methods are supposed to be adequate to what is under study, approaches to defining and assessing the quality of qualitative research (still) have to be discussed in specific ways that are appropriate for qualitative research and even for specific approaches in qualitative research.

Scope of *The SAGE Qualitative Research Kit*

- *Designing Qualitative Research* (Uwe Flick) gives a brief introduction to qualitative research from the point of view of how to plan and design a concrete study using qualitative research in one way or the other. It is intended to outline a framework for the other books in *The Sage Qualitative Research*

Kit by focusing on how-to-do problems and on how to solve such problems in the research process. The book will address issues of constructing a research design in qualitative research; it will outline stepping-stones in making a research project work and will discuss practical problems such as resources in qualitative research but also more methodological issues like quality of qualitative research and also ethics. This framework is spelled out in more details in the other books in the *Kit*.

- Three books are devoted to collecting or producing data in qualitative research. They take up the issues briefly outlined in the first book and approach them in a much more detailed and focused way for the specific method. First, *Doing Interviews* (Steinar Kvale) addresses the theoretical, epistemological, ethical and practical issues of interviewing people about specific issues or their life history. *Doing Ethnographic and Observational Research* (Michael Angrosino) focuses on the second major approach to collecting and producing qualitative data. Here again practical issues (like selecting sites, methods of collecting data in ethnography, special problems of analyzing them) are discussed in the context of more general issues (ethics, representations, quality and adequacy of ethnography as an approach). In *Doing Focus Groups* (Rosaline Barbour) the third of the most important qualitative methods of producing data is presented. Here again we find a strong focus on how-to-do issues of sampling, designing and analyzing the data and on how to produce them in focus groups.
- Three further volumes are devoted to analyzing specific types of qualitative data. *Using Visual Data in Qualitative Research* (Marcus Banks) extends the focus to the third type of qualitative data (beyond verbal data coming from interviews and focus groups and observational data). The use of visual data has not only become a major trend in social research in general, but confronts researchers with new practical problems in using them and analyzing them and produces new ethical issues. In *Analyzing Qualitative Data* (Graham Gibbs), several practical approaches and issues of making sense of any sort of qualitative data are addressed. Special attention is paid to practices of coding, of comparing and of using computer-assisted qualitative data analysis. Here, the focus is on verbal data like interviews, focus groups or biographies. *Doing Conversation, Discourse and Document Analysis* (Tim Rapley) extends this focus to different types of data, relevant for analyzing discourses. Here, the focus is on existing material (like documents) and on recording everyday conversations and on finding traces of discourses. Practical issues such as generating an archive, transcribing video materials and of how to analyze discourses with such types of data are discussed.
- *Managing Quality in Qualitative Research* (Uwe Flick) takes up the issue of quality in qualitative research, which has been briefly addressed in specific contexts in other books in the *Kit*, in a more general way. Here, quality is looked at from the angle of using or reformulating existing or defining

new criteria for qualitative research. This book will examine the ongoing debates about what should count as defining 'quality' and validity in qualitative methodologies and will examine the many strategies for promoting and managing quality in qualitative research. Special attention is paid to the strategy of triangulation in qualitative research and to the use of quantitative research in the context of promoting the quality of qualitative research.

Before I go on to outline the focus of this book and its role in the *Kit*, I would like to thank some people at SAGE who were important in making this *Kit* happen. Michael Carmichael suggested this project to me some time ago and was very helpful with his suggestions in the beginning. Patrick Brindle took over and continued this support, as did Vanessa Harwood and Jeremy Toynsoe in making books out of the manuscripts we provided.

About this book
Uwe Flick

In the history of qualitative research as well as in its recent development, ethnography and participant observation have played a major role. Much of the knowledge about field relations, about openness and directedness towards a field and its members is known from research in ethnography. Although it is closely linked to the method of participant observation, was based on it or maybe has replaced it more recently, ethnography always included a variety of methods of data collection. Quite often we find combinations of observation, participation, more or less formal interviewing and the use of documents and other traces of events in ethnography. At the same time, not every relevant issue is accessible for ethnography and participant observation. Sampling in this context is less focused on people to select for the research than on selecting fields or institutions, or more generally, sites for observation. Towards the end of the twentieth century, methodological discussions in ethnography have more and more shifted from issues of data collection and finding a role in the field to questions of writing about and reporting from the field, the research and the experiences in it. Analyzing ethnographic data is often oriented towards searching for patterns of behaviors, interactions and practices.

In this book such key topics of ethnographic and observational research are unfolded in some detail. Whereas the other books are more focused on verbal data like interviews (Kvale 2007) or focus groups (Barbour 2007) or concentrating on analyzing conversations (Rapley 2007) or images (Banks 2007), this book brings the pragmatics of field research into the scope of *The SAGE Qualitative Research Kit*. At the same time, it can be complemented by more detailed analysis of using these sources (from interviews to visual data) in the more general context of ethnography. The books on analyzing data (Gibbs 2007), designs and quality in qualitative research (Flick 2007a, b) add some extra context to what is outlined here in some detail. Together these books and this one allow deciding when to use ethnography and observation and provide a methodological and theoretical basis for using this strategy in the field. Here, the exemplary studies repeatedly used for illustration in this book are helpful for seeing ethnography not so much as a method but more as a strategy and when it is appropriate to issues and fields under study.

▌▌ Preface

The term 'ethnography' refers to both a method of research and the product of that research (Agar, 1980).

The ethnographic method involves the collection of information about the material products, social relationships, beliefs, and values of a community. Data collection relies on a variety of techniques; indeed, it is desirable to approach the collection of data from as many different perspectives as possible, the better to confirm that things really are as they seem.

The ethnographic product is a report that incorporates the information collected by the ethnographic method into a holistic description of the culture of the community. The report has traditionally taken the form of a written monograph, but it may also be a collection of photos, a movie or video, a museum display, a website, or even a work of literature (novel, play, short story, poem) or artistic performance (dance, song cycle).

Ethnographic research was pioneered by anthropologists in the late nineteenth and early twentieth centuries, although it has since become part of the toolkit of qualitative researchers in many disciplines, including sociology, social psychology, communication, education, business, and health. Because ethnography seeks a detailed and comprehensive description of a people, it is typically conducted by researchers who are able to spend an extended amount of time in the community they are studying (usually referred to as a *field site*). Their research is thus known as fieldwork.

Ethnographic fieldworkers often become *participant observers* who balance the objective collection of data with the subjective insights that result from an ongoing association with the people whose lives they seek to understand. Ethnographic methods can certainly be used by researchers who are not participant observers, but in this book we will emphasize the fieldwork of those who are.

This book will:

- introduce the reader to the variety of data collection techniques associated with ethnographic research, particularly as it is conducted by participant observer field researchers; and
- guide the reader through the process of ethnographic research, from site selection through the production of a final report.

This book includes some special features:

- There will be a consideration of the ethical implications of ethnographic research. Field researchers must always be aware of the delicate balance inherent in being both engaged participants in community activities and objective observers of those activities. Moreover, ethnographic research does not always clearly fit into the clinical/experimental model of research envisioned by most institutional ethical review panels; we will therefore consider ways of dealing with questions of informed consent and confidentiality when conducting research in real-life communities (as opposed to laboratories).
- There will be a discussion of ethnography for the new millennium. People no longer live exclusively in small, self-contained, localized communities. They are involved in extended global networks facilitated by advanced communication and transportation technology. We will therefore discuss some ways in which traditional ethnographic methods may be adapted to research in the 'virtual' communities of the global, cyberspace age.
- The text will be supported by illustrative case material. It is one thing to *tell* readers how to do ethnographic research; it is quite another to *show* them how the idealized guidelines of a textbook can be translated into real-life research situations. To that end, each didactic segment of the book will be illustrated by brief descriptions of the author's own fieldwork, comparing and contrasting a research project conducted in a traditional community in another part of the world with one conducted close to home.

Further reading

This is a classic introductory text for ethnography:
Agar, M. (1980) *The Professional Stranger: An Informal Introduction to Ethnography*. San Diego: Academic Press.

1
Introduction: ethnography and participant observation

Chapter objectives
After reading this chapter you should

- know working definitions of our key terms: ethnography and participant observation;
- see the results from comparing and contrasting the use of the term 'ethnography' as both method and product; and
- know about participant observation as a style that may be adopted by ethnographic researchers and as context to which a variety of data collection techniques can be adapted.

A brief history of ethnographic research

Ethnography literally means a description of a people. It is important to understand that ethnography deals with people in the collective sense, not with individuals. As such, it is a way of studying people in organized, enduring groups, which may be referred to as communities or societies. The distinctive way of life that characterizes such a group is its culture. The study of culture involves an examination of the group's learned and shared behaviors, customs, and beliefs.

The ethnographic approach to the study of human groups began with anthropologists in the late 19th and early 20th centuries who were convinced that the armchair speculations of earlier social philosophers were inadequate for understanding the way real people actually lived. They came to the conclusion that only in the field could a scholar truly encounter the dynamics of the lived human experience. Those in Britain (and other parts of the British Empire, later the Commonwealth, such as Australia and India) developed one form of ethnographic research. It reflected their fieldwork in areas then still under colonial control, societies such as those in Africa or the Pacific that seemed to be preserved in their traditional forms. In retrospect, of course, we can see that the colonial encounter drastically changed many of those societies, but a hundred years ago it was possible to look at them as being relatively untouched by the outside. The British therefore emphasized a study of the enduring institutions of society; that approach came to be called social anthropology. The two most influential social anthropologists of the British school were A.R. Radcliffe-Brown and Bronislaw Malinowski (McGee and Warms, 2003, see especially pp. 153–215).

By contrast, anthropologists in the United States were interested in studying native American people whose traditional ways of life had by then already been drastically altered, if not completely destroyed. The US anthropologists could not assume that native people lived in the context of social institutions that represented their indigenous condition. If culture could not be found in those institutions, then it would have to be reconstructed through the historical memory of the survivors. American anthropology thus came to be referred to as cultural anthropology. The most influential American cultural anthropologist was Franz Boas, who trained a whole generation of American scholars, including Alfred Kroeber, Ruth Benedict, Margaret Mead, and Robert Lowie (McGee and Warms, 2003, see especially pp. 128–52).

Malinowski and Boas were both strong advocates of field-based research and both advocated what has come to be known as participant observation, a way of conducting research that places the researcher in the midst of the community he or she is studying. Because of complications arising out of international conditions during the First World War, Malinowski, who was conducting a field study of the Trobriand Islands (Western Pacific), was stranded at his field site for four years. Although it has rarely been possible to duplicate that unplanned feat, Malinowski's Trobriand ethnography has often been held up as the gold standard for the long-term total immersion of a researcher in the society under study.

The pioneers of field-based research believed that they were adhering to a method consonant with that of the natural sciences, but the fact that they were living in the very communities they were analyzing introduced a level of subjectivity into their analysis that was at variance with the scientific method as commonly understood.

Beginning in the 1920s, sociologists at the University of Chicago adapted the anthropologists' ethnographic field research methods to the study of social groups in 'modern' communities in the United States (Bogdan and Biklen, 2003). The influence of this 'Chicago school' ultimately affected such fields as education, business, public health, nursing, and mass communications.

Sociocultural theory and ethnographic research

As the ethnographic method has spread across disciplines, it has become associated with a wide variety of theoretical orientations:

- structure-functionalism
- symbolic interactionism
- feminism
- Marxism
- ethnomethodology
- critical theory
- cultural studies
- postmodernism

Structure-functionalism

This was the dominant school of anthropology in Britain for much of the twentieth century, and it has long had philosophical and methodological links to sociology in both the United Kingdom and the United States. Structure-functionalism is characterized by the following basic concepts:

- The *organic analogy*, which means that society is thought of as analogous to a biological organism with structures and functions parallelling those of the physical organ systems. Each social institution, like each organ system, has a particular role to play in keeping the entire society/organism alive, but no one of them can operate optimally unless properly connected to all the others.
- A *natural science orientation*, which means that society is supposed to be studied empirically, the better to uncover its underlying patterns and overall order.
- A *narrowed conceptual field*, which means that structure-functionalists prefer to focus on society and its subsystems (e.g. the family, economy, political institutions, beliefs); they have paid comparatively little attention to art, language, personality development, technology, and the natural environment.
- A sense of *universality*, which means that all social institutions and their respective functions are assumed to be found in equivalent structures in all societies.

- The pre-eminence of *kinship studies*, which means that family ties are presumed to be the 'glue' that holds societies together; in modern societies, other institutions take on roles equivalent to the traditional family, but presumably always do so on the model of the family.
- A tendency toward *equilibrium*, which means that societies are assumed to be characterized by harmony and internal consistency; disruptions or anomalies are ultimately corrected by mechanisms existing within the society itself. This assumption leads to a tendency to see societies as somewhat *static* in their overall balance, and hence to a disinclination to study historical factors making for change in social life.

In terms of method, the structure-functionalists are strong advocates of fieldwork based on participant observation, which, in the ideal at least, is a long-term commitment, since the underlying order of a society can only be revealed by patient immersion in the lives of the people under study. A major emphasis of ethnographic fieldwork in the structure-functionalist tradition is the linkage of rules of behavior (norms) with behavior itself; disparities between what people said they ought to do and what they actually did are de-emphasized. Such an assumption works best in small, relatively homogeneous communities; hence the structure-functionalists have favored fieldwork in traditional, isolated societies or in bounded neighborhoods in modern urban areas.

Structure-functionalists approach ethnography as if it were a purely empirical exercise. People's beliefs and behaviors are considered to be real *social facts*; they are 'data' that are to be collected by objective researchers with a minimum of interpretation. Although they prefer to work with qualitative data (as opposed to numerical data generated by surveys and so forth), they uphold the scientific nature of ethnography because their data collection is in service to a view of order in social life, the pre-eminence of facts over interpretation, and by the notion that every event has a function within a coherent system.

Because kinship is seen to be the key to social organization, the structure-functionalists are particularly fond of using genealogical methods to reconstruct and illuminate all aspects of a society. They also tend to use the method of the *interview schedule*, which means that questions are asked verbally by a researcher, who fills in the answers; this approach differs from that of the questionnaire, which is distributed to respondents who then fill it out themselves. In the ideal, all interviews are done in the indigenous language, although this stipulation must sometimes be realized in the form of paid translators.

Ethnographic research in this tradition thus relies heavily on the personal interactions of researchers and their 'subjects'. While the data are believed to be objectively real, the circumstances in which those data are collected cannot be easily replicated. Hence, the structure-functionalist tradition of research emphasizes *validity* over 'reliability' (the latter being a criterion of the scientific method emphasizing replicable experiments).

Ethnography in this tradition requires lengthy immersion in particular societies. Given the logistical constraints on carrying out that mission, it is usually not possible to conduct genuinely cross-cultural research. A cross-cultural picture might emerge from the gradual accretion of particularistic studies, but the use of a standardized research design carried out by researchers simultaneously in several different locations is not a common practice. One of the perhaps unintended consequences of this tendency is an overemphasis of the perceived uniqueness of each society.

Structure-functionalist ethnography serves an *inductive* rather than a *deductive* agenda for scientific inquiry. That is, researchers begin with a particular tribe, village, community, or neighborhood that they are interested in learning about, rather than with a theory, model, or hypothesis to test. It is considered appropriate for themes or patterns to emerge from the data collected in the course of fieldwork. (See Turner, 1978, pp. 19–120, for a more complete treatment of the history, philosophy, and methods of functionalism.)

Symbolic interactionism

This orientation has been very popular in sociology and social psychology and it also has some adherents in anthropology. Unlike those social scientists who might seem to overemphasize the role of culture in 'shaping' human behavior, interactionists prefer to see people as active agents rather than as interchangeable parts in a large organism, passively acted upon by forces external to themselves. Society is not a set of interlocking institutions, as the structure-functionalists might have thought, but an ever-changing kaleidoscope of individuals interacting with each other. As the nature of those interactions shifts, so society is constantly changing, too. Interactionism is therefore a dynamic rather than a static approach to the study of social life.

There are several varieties of interactionism (four, seven, or eight, depending on which account one reads), but all of them share some basic assumptions:

- people live in a world of learned meanings, which are encoded as *symbols* and which are shared through interactions in a given social group;
- symbols are motivational in that they impel people to carry out their activities;
- the human mind itself grows and changes in response to the quality and extent of interactions in which the individual engages;
- the *self* is a social construct – our notion of who we are develops only in the course of interacting with others.

Ethnographic fieldwork in the interactionist tradition is geared toward uncovering the meanings social actors attach to their actions. The structure-functionalist emphasis on behavior as a set of objective facts is replaced by a more subjective delineation of how people understand what they do. Some interactionists refer to

5

this process as 'sympathetic introspection', while others prefer to use the German word *verstehen* in homage to the great German sociologist Max Weber, who introduced the concept into modern social science discourse. In either case, the implication is that the researcher must become immersed in the world of his or her subjects; he or she cannot be a neutral observer of their activities, but must become subjectively one with them. The key to interactionist ethnography is the uncovering of the system of symbols that gives meaning to what people think and do.

One particularly influential interactionist is the sociologist Erving Goffman, who developed what he called a *dramaturgical* approach to the study of interactions. He was concerned with how people act and form relationships, because he believed that these processes helped people achieve meaning in their lives. His research often involved descriptions of how people construct their 'presentations of self' and then perform those presentations in front of others. Goffman suggested that there is intentionality behind such performances, in that they are engaged in with an eye toward making the best possible impression (as the 'actor' understands it) in the view of significant others. They become not simply 'role makers', but active 'role players'.

Because of their interest in the nature of interactions, symbolic interactionists have devoted considerable attention to the interactions that are typical of ethnographic fieldwork itself. In a sense, they have been led to conduct an ethnographic study of the process of doing ethnography. Briefly summarizing a very large body of literature on this topic, we may say that ethnographers' interactive roles fall along a continuum with four main points: (a) the complete participant (the researcher is totally immersed in the community and does not disclose his or her research agenda); (b) the participant-as-observer (the researcher is immersed in the community but is known to be conducting research and has permission to do so); (c) the observer-as-participant (the researcher is somewhat detached from the community, interacting with it only on specific occasions, perhaps to conduct interviews or attend organized functions); and (d) the complete observer (the researcher collects completely objective data about the community from afar without becoming involved in its activities or announcing his or her presence). Each of these roles is potentially useful depending on circumstances, although tilting toward the 'participant' end of the continuum would seem to serve the goals of symbolic interactionism most effectively. (See Herman and Reynolds, 1994, for a more complete review of the theory and methods of the interactionist approach. See Gold, 1958, for the classic exposition of researcher roles alluded to in this section.)

Feminism

This approach to scholarship has in recent decades become prominent in all of the social sciences (and humanities as well, for that matter). Although linked with the sociopolitical movement for women's rights, scholarly feminism is not the concern solely of women researchers; it represents a general approach to the study of the human social condition. Several basic principles characterize feminism in the modern social science context:

- the assumption that all social relations are *gendered*, which means that a consciousness of gender is one of the elementary factors determining a person's social status;
- the suggestion (not universally shared among feminists, it should be noted) that there is some sort of female 'essence' characterized by fundamental qualities of nurturance, caring, and a preference for cooperation over competition. This essence is expressed in different ways in different cultures, but it is recognized in some way in all societies. The reason this suggestion is not universally accepted is because there is a countervailing proposition, to wit:
- the behaviors that are considered typical or one gender or another are socially learned rather than biologically inbred; this does not make them any less important or influential in the way people act and think, but it does move the inquiry away from the biogenetic to the sociocultural perspective. Regardless of whether gender is 'essential' or socially learned, there is perceived to be
- a universal *sexual asymmetry*; even in those rare societies in which men and women are considered to be more or less equal partners, there is a recognition that men and women are different from each other, either because of innate biology or because of differential processes of *socialization* (the ways in which we learn to take on the behaviors our society tells us are appropriate).

A feminist approach has certain clear implications for the conduct of ethnographic research. For one thing, feminists tend to reject the traditional separation of a researcher and her or his 'subjects'. Such a distinction is seen to reflect the traditional categories of science which, whatever else may be said for it, has long been used as a tool of oppression. Traditional scientific research, with its emphasis on testing, operational definitions, scales, and rules, is said to have served mainly the interest of those in power, which, in most cases, did not include women. The detached researcher in control of all the elements of a research project was an authority figure par excellence, and his power was only enhanced by the enforcement of norms of objectivity and neutrality in the conduct of research. Feminists seek to de-center this relationship by a closer identification of the researcher with the community under study. Value-neutrality as a scientific ideal is rejected by feminists, because they actively and explicitly seek to promote the interests of women.

By the same token, the orderly, coherent models of social equilibrium favored by the structure-functionalists (among others) are set aside in favor of a view of social life as sometimes disorderly, incomplete, fragmented. To that end, feminist researchers look to a form of ethnography that allows for empathy, subjectivity, and dialogue, the better to explore the inner worlds of women, even to the point of helping them articulate (and hence overcome) their oppression. The traditional 'interview' (which implicitly casts the researcher in a role of power) is also rejected in favor of a more egalitarian dialogue, often embodied in the form of the *life history* in which a person is encouraged to tell her own story in her own way and in her own terms, with minimal prompting by the researcher. Ethnography based in the life-history approach is seen as a way to 'give voice' to people historically relegated to the margins of society (and social analysis); it is also a way to preserve the wholeness of individuals, as opposed to other interviewing techniques that tend to separate them into analytical component parts. (See Morgen, 1989, for further insights into the emerging feminist perspective.)

Marxism

Marxism has had a huge impact on the study of history, economics, and political science, but its influence on those disciplines that deal with human social behavior (anthropology, sociology, social psychology) has been somewhat indirect. It is rare to find social scientists representing these disciplines who are Marxist in the fullest philosophical sense, and fewer still (especially in the years since the fall of the Soviet Union) who see Marxism per se as an ideology that might fruitfully underpin an agenda for social reform. Nonetheless, several important elements of Marxism remain very much in the thick of current discourse about society and culture.

Perhaps the most prominent Marxist-derived concept is that of *conflict*. Conflict theoreticians propose that society is defined by its interest groups, which are necessarily in competition with each other for basic resources, which may be economic, political, and/or social in nature. Unlike the functionalists, who see society as governed by some sort of core value system and who thus view conflict as an anomaly that must ultimately be overcome so that the society can re-establish equilibrium, conflict theoreticians believe that conflict is intrinsic to human interaction; indeed, it is the very thing that brings about social change. For Marx and his followers, group conflict is embedded in the institution of *social class*. Classes arise out of a fundamental division of labor within a society; they represent networks of people defined by their status position within a hierarchical structure. In the Marxist tradition, social change comes about because there is a *dialectic* process – the contradictions between and among competing social classes are resolved through conflicts of interest. Like feminism, Marxism (or, more broadly, conflict theory) focuses on issues of inequality and oppression, although the latter prefer to think in terms of socioeconomic categories like class, rather than sociocultural ones like gender as the basis of conflict.

Contemporary Marxist scholars are particularly interested in the question of *colonialism* and how that political-economic institution distorted relations between 'core' states (those that maintain a 'hegemonic' control over the production and distribution of the world's goods and services, and that therefore have a near-monopoly on political and military power) and those on the 'periphery' (the ones that produce mainly raw materials and are thus perpetually dependent on those in control). This imbalance persists even though colonialism as an institution has disappeared in the formal sense. 'World systems theory' is one body of literature that addresses these issues of hegemony and dependency.

Modern-day students of political economy are particularly interested in what is sometimes called *material relations*, which entails a study of groups interacting with nature in the course of production, interacting with one another in relations of production that differentiate them into classes, and interacting with the 'cores', which use their coercive power to shape both production and social relations. This perspective shifts the focus away from self-contained societies, communities, neighborhoods, and so forth, and toward a consideration of the ways in which local groups are part of both regional and international flows of people, goods, services, and power. In order to understand what is going on in any one locality, it is necessary to place that society/community/culture in the context of large-scale political and economic areas in which they are influenced by other societies and cultures. The emphasis thus is *trans-cultural* rather than particular-istic in nature.

Given these assumptions, it would seem that the somewhat subjective, person-alized style of ethnographic research would not be a comfortable fit for conflict theoreticians or those engaged in neo-Marxist political economic research. However, it is important to note that traditional ethnographic methods may be deployed in the study of local communities, as has long been the case. The cru-cial difference, however, is that such ethnographic studies are designed to demon-strate not the autonomy and near-uniqueness of those communities, but their linkages to other communities that ultimately form global systems. Moreover, the neo-Marxist ethnographer would be inclined to look for evidence of class struc-tures and the conflicts and contradictions inherent within them, even in societies that on the surface may appear to be egalitarian, non-hierarchical, and in a state seemingly approaching equilibrium. (See Wolf, 1982, for a grand exposition of the principles of neo-Marxist political economy and the ways in which traditional research about culture can be transformed to serve the purposes of this theoreti-cal perspective.)

Ethnomethodology

This approach to the study of human behavior has been particularly influential in sociology. The aim of ethnomethodologists has been to explain how a group's sense of reality is constructed, maintained, and changed. It is based on two principal propositions:

- Human interaction is *reflexive*, which means that people interpret cues (such as words, gestures, body language, the use of space and time) in such a way as to uphold a common vision of reality; evidence that seems to contradict the common vision is either rejected or somehow rationalized into the prevailing system.
- Information is *indexed*, which means that it has meaning within a particular context; it is thus important to know the biographies of the interacting parties, their avowed purposes, and their past interactions in order to understand what is going on in a particular observed situation.

Ethnomethodological research assumes that social order is maintained by the use of techniques that allow those involved in interactions the sense that they share a common reality. Moreover, the actual content of that reality is less important than the fact that those involved accept the techniques designed to sustain the interaction. Some of the more important techniques – ones that ethnomethodologists look for when they study social settings – are:

- *The search for the 'normal form'*, which means that if the parties to the interaction begin to feel that they may not actually agree about what is going on, they will offer gestures that cue each other to return to the presumed 'norm' in their context.
- *The reliance on a 'reciprocity of perspective'*, which means that people actively communicate the belief (accepted as fact) that their experiences are interchangeable, even though they implicitly realize that they are 'coming from different places'.
- *The use of the 'et cetera principle'*, which means that in any interaction much is left unsaid, so that parties to the interaction must either fill in or wait for information needed to make sense of the other's words or actions; they implicitly agree not to interrupt to ask explicitly for clarification.

These techniques are almost always subconscious in nature and, as such, are taken for granted by members of a society. The job of the researcher is thus to uncover those covert meanings. Since it is pointless to ask people to elucidate actions they are not consciously aware of, ethnomethodologists favor observational to interview-based research. Indeed, they have refined observational methods down to the most minute 'micro exchanges', such as the analysis of conversations. Some ethnomethodologists contend that language is the fundamental base of the social order, since it is the vehicle of the communication that sustains that order in the first place.

Ethnomethodologists use the ethnographic method in order to grapple with that which is most readily observable, which is taken to be that which is most 'real'. In most cases, this reality is given substance by the attempts of interacting individuals to persuade each other that the situation in which they find themselves is both orderly and appropriate to the social setting at hand. What is 'really real', as some analysts have put it, is the methods people use in order to construct, maintain, and sometimes subtly alter for each other a sense of order. The content of what they are saying or doing is less real than the techniques they use to convince each other that it is real. The implication is that ethnography is not used to study some large, transcendent system like 'culture' or 'society', since such abstractions can never truly order people's behavior. Rather, ethnographic research is designed to uncover how people convince each other that there really is such a thing as 'society' or 'culture' in the sense of coherent norms guiding their interaction. There is no predetermined 'sense of order' that makes society possible; rather, it is the capacity of individuals to create and use methods to persuade each other that there is a real social world to which they both belong – and to do so both actively and continually – that is the crux of the matter.

The job of ethnography, then, for the ethnomethodologists is not to answer the question, 'What is "culture"?' or 'What is "society"?' but to answer the question, 'How do people convince themselves that "culture" and "society" are viable propositions?' (See Mehan and Wood, 1975, for a clear exposition of the ethnomethodological position.)

Critical theory

This general term covers a variety of approaches to the study of contemporary society and culture. The linking theme is, as the title implies, the use of social science to challenge the assumptions of the dominant institutions of society. Feminism and Marxism, to be sure, join in this endeavor, and may be considered as variants of 'critical theory', albeit ones with their own distinctive histories and bodies of literature. In this section, however, we can consider those researchers who use ethnographic methods in order to study and influence public policy and to participate actively in political movements for social change, often playing an advocacy role that steps well beyond traditional notions of researcher neutrality.

The main philosophical approach of critical ethnographers is the development of 'multiple standpoint epistemologies', which is an explicit challenge to the traditional assumption that there was an objective, universally understood definition of what constitutes a culture. When a structure-functionalist, for example, described a particular community, his or her understanding was that this description could have been generated by any well-trained researcher and that it represented a general consensus on the part of the people in the community that this was the way things were. A multiple standpoint perspective, however, is based on the assumption that not only will there inevitably be different bodies of opinion within the community, but that different ethnographers, who bring their own baggage with them so to speak, will produce different images of what they have observed. The different bodies of opinion may not be in explicit conflict with one another, as in Marxist theory, but they certainly do not make for cultural or social homogeneity. For the critical theorist, then, it is important to know which segment of the society is being studied by which ethnographer. A portrait that purports to be a more general view is intrinsically suspect.

Critical theorists have therefore come to favor a style of ethnographic research that is *dialogic, dialectical,* and *collaborative.* A dialogic ethnography is one that is not based on the traditional power relationships of interviewer and 'subject'. Rather the researcher enters into give-and-take conversations with the people of the community. The sense of a 'dialectic' perspective is that truth emerges from the confluence of divergent opinions, values, beliefs, and behaviors, not from some false homogenization imposed from the outside. Moreover, the people of the community are not 'subjects' at all; they are active collaborators in the research effort. Indeed, in certain forms of critical research (particularly that known as *participatory action research*), every effort is made to involve the community as active partners in the design and implementation of the research. In the ideal, the main task of the researcher is to train members of the community in the techniques of research so that they can do it for themselves. All of these tendencies make for a style of research that is deliberately confrontational; in both the way the research is conducted and in the findings derived from the research, there is an explicit challenge to the status quo. (See Marcus, 1999, for a selection of readings on the critical approach in anthropology and related disciplines.)

Cultural studies

Another form of critical theory that has emerged in recent years as a substantial research focus of its own is *cultural studies*, which is a field of research that examines how the lives of people are shaped by structures that have been handed down historically. Cultural studies scholars are first of all concerned with *cultural texts,* institutions such as the mass media and manifestations of popular culture that represent convergences of history, ideology, and subjective experience. The aim of ethnography with respect to cultural texts is to discern how the 'audience' relates to such texts, and to determine how hegemonic meanings are produced, distributed, and consumed.

An important feature of cultural studies is that researchers are expected to be *self-reflexive,* which means that they are as much concerned with who they are (with respect to their gender, race, ethnicity, social class, sexual orientation, age, and so forth) as determinants of how they see culture and society as they are with the artifacts of culture and society per se. Traditional ethnographers were, in a way, non-persons – extensions of their tape recorders, as it were. Cultural studies ethnographers, by contrast, are hyper-conscious of their own biographies, which are considered to be legitimate parts of the story.

Cultural studies is by definition an interdisciplinary field, and so its methods derive from anthropology, sociology, psychology, and history. Some have criticized this school for favoring 'theory' – producing their analyses on the basis of abstract conceptual frameworks in preference to doing fieldwork. While this may be true in some instances, it is also true that fundamental methods of observation, interviewing, and archival research that might be used by any other social researcher are also part of the active toolkit of cultural studies scholars. However, the latter join with other critical theorists in insisting that such methods be put to the service of a sustained challenge to the social and cultural status quo. Whereas other critical scholars might prefer to use their research to advocate for specific policy outcomes, cultural studies scholars are more inclined to think in terms of a general critique of culture itself. (See Storey, 1998, for an exposition of the main concepts and approaches of cultural studies.)

Postmodernism

Several of these more recently developed approaches have also been lumped together under the label *postmodernism*. 'Modernism' was the movement in the social sciences that sought to emulate the scientific method in its objectivity and search for general patterns. 'Postmodernism', therefore, is all that challenges that *positivistic* program. Postmodernism embraces the plurality of experience, argues against the reliance on general 'laws' of human behavior, and situates all social, cultural, and historical knowledge in the contexts shaped by gender, race, and class.

Although 'postmodernism' has come to mean many things to different analysts, there are several principles that seem to hold across the vast spectrum of research so identified:

- Traditional centers of authority are explicitly challenged; this attitude is directed not only at the institutions of hegemonic dominance in society at large, but also at the pillars of the scientific establishment. Postmodernists reject the presumption of scientists to 'speak for' those whom they study.
- Human life is fundamentally *dialogical* and *polyvocal*, which means that no community can be described as a homogeneous entity in equilibrium; society is by definition a set of competing centers of interest who speak with many voices about what their culture is and is not; by extension, ethnographic research must take into account the multiple voices with which communities actually speak. 'Culture' and 'society' are concepts arrived at through a process of *social construction* rather than objective entities – although this does not make them any less 'real'.
- The ethnographic product is less an objective scientific document than a kind of literary text; it is produced as much through imaginative use of such literary devices as metaphors and symbols as it is through neutral reportage. Moreover, that ethnographic text need not be restricted to the traditional forms of the scholarly monograph, journal article, or conference presentation; rather, it may be embodied in film, drama, poetry, novels, pictorial displays, music,

13

and so forth. An important corollary to this proposition is the assumption that the ethnographer is an 'author' of the text – he or she figures in the story as much more than a simple, neutral reporter of objective 'data.' (See Clifford and Marcus, 1986, and Marcus and Fischer, 1986, two widely influential expositions of the postmodernist position.)

- There is a shift in emphasis away from discerning patterns of determination and causality and toward the explication of *meaning*, which requires a process of *interpretation.*
- The study of any one culture, society, or any other such phenomenon is essentially *relativistic* – the forces that shape that phenomenon are distinctively different from those that produce others, such that generalizations about social and cultural process are bound to be misleading.

Ethnography: basic principles

Despite this diversity of positions from which ethnographers may derive, we may still highlight a few important features that link the many and varied approaches:

- A search for *patterns* proceeds from the careful observations of lived behavior and from detailed interviews with people in the community under study. When ethnographers speak about 'culture' or 'society' or 'community', it is important to keep in mind that they are speaking in terms that are generalized abstractions based on numerous bits of data in ways that make sense to the ethnographer who has a global overview of the social or cultural whole that people living in it may lack.
- Ethnographers must pay careful attention to the process of field research. Attention must always be paid to the ways in which one gains entry to the field site, establishes rapport with the people living there, and comes to be a participating member of that group.

Definitions

So at this point we can say that

> ethnography is the art and science of describing a human group – its institutions, interpersonal behaviors, material productions, and beliefs.

Although developed as a way of studying small-scale, non-literate, traditional societies and of reconstructing their cultural traditions, ethnography is now practiced in all sorts of social settings. In whatever setting,

> ethnographic researchers are primarily concerned with the routine, everyday lives of the people they study.

Ethnographers collect data about the lived human experience in order to discern *predictable patterns* rather than to describe every conceivable instance of interaction or production.

Ethnography is conducted on-site and the ethnographer is, as much as possible, a subjective *participant* in the lives of those under study, as well as an objective *observer* of those lives.

Ethnography as method

The ethnographic method is different from other ways of conducting social science research.

- It is *field-based* (conducted in the settings in which real people actually live, rather than in laboratories where the researcher controls the elements of the behaviors to be observed or measured).
- It is *personalized* (conducted by researchers who are in day-to-day, face-to-face contact with the people they are studying and who are thus both participants in and observers of the lives under study).
- It is *multifactorial* (conducted through the use of two or more data collection techniques – which may be qualitative or quantitative in nature – in order to *triangulate* on a conclusion, which may be said to be strengthened by the multiple ways in which it was reached; see also Flick, 2007b, for a discussion of this issue).
- It requires a *long-term* commitment (i.e. it is conducted by researchers who intend to interact with the people they are studying for an extended period of time – although the exact time frame may vary anywhere from several weeks to a year or more).
- It is *inductive* (conducted in such a way as to use an accumulation of descriptive detail to build toward general patterns or explanatory theories rather than structured to test hypotheses derived from existing theories or models).
- It is *dialogic* (conducted by researchers whose conclusions and interpretations can be commented upon by those under study even as they are being formed).
- It is *holistic* (conducted so as to yield the fullest possible portrait of the group under study).

Ethnography as product

The results of some forms of ethnographic data collection may be reducible to tables, graphs, or charts, but on the whole the finished ethnographic report takes the form of a *narrative*, a kind of extended story whose main goal is to draw the reader into a vicarious experience of the community in which the ethnographer has lived and interacted. The most common form of narrative is rendered in prose, in which case it often borrows (consciously or not) some of the literary techniques common to storytelling of any kind. (If the ethnographer makes the choice to tell the story in forms other than prose, then the resulting 'narrative' will be similarly influenced by the artistic conventions of visual art, dance, film, or whatever.)

There are many different ways in which an ethnographer can tell a story, three categories of which seem to be most common:

- Stories told in a *realistic mode* are de-personalized, objectively rendered portraits provided by an emotionally neutral analyst – even if he or she was an emotionally engaged participant during the conduct of the research itself.
- Stories told in a *confessional mode* are those in which the ethnographer becomes a central player and the story of the community under study is explicitly told through his or her particular viewpoint.
- Stories told in an *impressionistic mode* openly embrace literary – or other appropriately artistic – devices, such as the use of dialogue, elaborate character sketches, evocative descriptions of landscape or décor, flashback or flashforward narrative structure, use of metaphors). (See van Maanen, 1988, for the classic exposition of these and other 'tales' of fieldwork.)

Regardless of the format of the narrative, any ethnographic report must somehow include several key points if it is to serve the purposes of science as well as of literature or art:

- First, there should be *an introduction* in which the reader's attention is captured and in which the researcher explains why his or her study has analytical value.
- Then there can be *a setting of the scene* in which the researcher describes the setting of the research and explains the ways in which he or she went about collecting data in that setting; many authors use the term *thick description* to indicate the way in which the scene is depicted (although the reader is urged to be cautious as this term is also used in various other ways that depart from our discussion in this section) – 'thick description' is the presentation of details, context, emotions, and the nuances of social relationships in order to evoke the 'feeling' of a scene and not just its surface attributes. (See Geertz, 1973, for the classic treatment of this issue and an elaboration of its ramifications for the conduct of ethnographic research.)
- Next comes *an analysis* in which the researcher draws the numerous descriptive details into a coherent set of social/cultural patterns that help the reader make sense of the people and their community, and that link this particular ethnographic study to those produced from other, somewhat similar communities.

- Finally, there is *a conclusion* in which the researcher summarizes the main points and suggests the contributions of this study to the wider body of knowledge.

Participant observation as style and context

It is certainly possible to use data collection techniques that are typical of ethnographic research (see Chapter 4) in ways that do not involve participant observation. For example, it may be more efficient in some cases to ask participants to write out (or tape record) their own autobiographies, rather than have those life stories collected by an on-site interviewer. But this book will be mainly concerned with those situations in which ethnographic method and product are associated with participant observation in the field setting.

In non-participant ethnography, the only thing that really matters is that prospective participants recognize the researcher as a legitimate scholar who has taken the necessary ethical precautions in structuring his or her research. Their willingness to participate is thus a kind of business arrangement. The researcher relates to them strictly *as* a researcher. But in participant observation, the people of the study community agree to the presence of the researcher among them as a neighbor and friend who also happens to be a researcher. The participant observer must thus make the effort to be acceptable as a person (which will mean different things in terms of behavior, living arrangements, and sometimes even appearance in different cultures) and not simply reputable as a scientist. He or she must thus adopt a style that is agreeable to most of the people among whom he or she proposes to live. As such, the participant observer cannot hope to control all the elements of research; he or she is dependent on the goodwill of the community (sometimes in a very literal sense, if it is a community in which the basic resources for living are scarce) and must make a tacit agreement to 'go with the flow', even if it doesn't work out according to a carefully prepared research design. As an acceptable neighbor and friend, the participant observer can go about the business of collecting data. But for our purposes in this book, remember that participant observation is not itself a 'method' of research – it is the behavioral context out of which an ethnographer uses defined techniques to collect data.

Key points

- Ethnographic research involves the holistic description of a people and their way of life.
- Ethnography was developed by anthropologists in the late nineteenth and early twentieth centuries for the study of small-scale, traditional, isolated societies, although it is now widely used by practitioners of many disciplines in all kinds of research settings.

- Ethnographic research is often conducted by scholars who are both subjective participants in the community under study and objective observers thereof.
- Ethnography is a *method* of research that seeks to define predictable patterns of group behavior. It is field-based, personalized, multifactorial, long-term, inductive, dialogic, and holistic in nature.
- Ethnography is also a *product* of research. It is a narrative about the study community that evokes the lived experience of that community and that invites the reader into a vicarious encounter with the people. The narrative is typically in prose, although it may also take other literary or artistic forms in order to convey the story. In all cases, it makes use of the literary and/or artistic conventions of the appropriate genre in order to tell the story in the most compelling way.
- Participant observation is not a method in itself, but rather a personal style adopted by field-based researchers who, having been accepted by the study community, are able to use a variety of data collection techniques to find out about the people and their way of life.

Further reading

These four books will give you more information of how to plan ethnographic research:

Agar, M. (1986) *Speaking of Ethnography*. Beverly Hills, CA: Academic Press.

Creswell, J.W. (1997) *Research Design: Qualitative and Quantitative Approaches*. Thousand Oaks, CA: Sage.

Fetterman, D.M. (1998) *Ethnography Step by Step* (2nd ed.). Thousand Oaks, CA: Sage.

Flick, U. (2007a) *Designing Qualitative Research* (Book 1 of *The SAGE Qualitative Research Kit*). London: Sage.

2
What kinds of topics can be effectively and efficiently studied by ethnographic methods?

Chapter objectives
After reading this chapter, you should know

- the main kinds of research problems that seem to call for choosing ethnographic methods; and
- the kinds of settings in which ethnographic methods might be most usefully applied.

Ethnographic methods: a general statement of utility

As noted in the previous chapter, ethnographic methods have been adopted by scholars from many academic disciplines and professional fields. There are, however, several characteristics that are typical of the situations that lend themselves to ethnographic research, regardless of discipline.

Illustrative ethnographic case studies

Throughout this book, two of the author's own field research projects will be used to illustrate major points. This material is offered as illustrative only, not as a model to be followed exactly. The two projects are meant only to help

---

Box 2.1   Utility of ethnographic methods

- In general, we use ethnographic methods to study social issues or behaviors that are not yet clearly understood. In such cases, entering the community with a detailed and quantifiable survey instrument would be premature. Ethnographic methods can help a researcher get the 'lay of the land' before honing in on particular issues with more statistically precise measures.
- Ethnographic methods are also worth using when getting the people's own perspective on issues is an important goal (rather than having them filtered through the outside researcher's perspective as represented by a survey or questionnaire developed on the basis of the existing research literature or on research in another, presumably similar community).

---

concretize otherwise abstract concepts. The author is a cultural anthropologist and so the projects tend to reflect an anthropological take on ethnographic research; readers from different disciplinary traditions will adapt the procedures according to the standards of their particular field of study.

The Trinidad Project

This project was conducted in a setting fairly typical of traditional cultural anthropology: a relatively well-bounded community with a strong self-image (and recognized as a definite community by outsiders) in a setting outside the United States. Since the early 1970s the author has been studying the descendants of people from India who were brought to various parts of the British Empire under a system of 'indenture' following the official end of slavery. Indentured laborers were not technically enslaved since the period of their bondage was limited by contract. After serving out their bonds, the laborers were free to leave the site of employment. During the period of the bond, however, conditions for the laborers were virtually identical with those that obtained during slavery. Although the Indians were in theory free to return to India, very few of them did so; the cost of the return passage was too great for many of them, and others believed that having crossed 'dark water' they had lost the traditional ties to the village system back home – they had, in effect, become ritually impure. So the vast majority of them remained in the areas in which they had been indentured. The author's particular interest has been in the West Indies, most specifically the island of Trinidad. Indians were brought to Trinidad to work on the sugar plantations. The Trinidad indenture lasted from 1837 through 1917. Descendants of the indentured Indians now constitute at least half the population of modern Trinidad; until very recently they have remained a largely agrarian population cut off from the island nation's political and economic mainstream. (See Angrosino, 1974, for a full account of the Trinidad project.)

The deinstitutionalization project

This study was conducted in a community closer to home. The author became interested in the situation of people with chronic mental illness and mental retardation who had been 'deinstitutionalized' beginning in the 1970s when advances in psychiatric medicine made it possible to treat their symptoms outside of hospitals. The deinstitutionalization movement had motives that were both humanitarian (allowing people to live in the community free from the rigors of institutional confinement) and economic (treating people on a case-by-case basis in the community was cheaper than 'warehousing' them for life). Some of the people affected by deinstitutionalization have made an adequate adjustment to life beyond the hospital, although others have fallen through the cracks in the complex health and human services systems and form the core of a homeless population visible in most major population centers. The author's research was centered on an agency in Florida that served a 'dually diagnosed' clientele – people with both severe mental illness and mental retardation – providing educational, vocational, and residential services. (See Angrosino, 1998, for a full account of this research project.)

Ethnographic methods: specific research problems

1. Ethnographic research is used to define a research problem

Certain well-established research topics attract the researcher because of their extensive bodies of associated literature, which make it possible to formulate reasonable working hypotheses that can then be tested using focused data collection tools. Other topics, by contrast, are more amorphous and need to be studied on the ground, as it were, before suitable hypotheses can be devised. It is for these latter topics that ethnographic methods are particularly well suited.

For example, in the Trinidad project, the Indian indenture in various parts of the old British Empire had been extensively studied by historians, economists, political scientists, sociologists, and social psychologists, as well as cultural anthropologists. Especially with regard to the West Indies, however, there had been at the time I began my research a tendency to focus on the most isolated and culturally traditional Indian communities. But Trinidad, with a modern industrial sector linked to the global petrochemical economy, provided many potential opportunities for Indians to break out of their traditional isolation. And indeed many of them had done so. Younger people were taking jobs in the non-agricultural sector, getting higher education, and living in homes outside the rural villages. But from what I had heard before doing field research of my own, I knew that the sense of Indian community identity remained very strong. What was going on in this transitional society? In what ways did Indians themselves understand the dynamic of living modern lives and yet defining themselves in terms of cultural tradition?

In the deinstitutionalization project, people who are mentally challenged have obvious difficulties when it comes to negotiating the complexities of everyday life. Such scholarly literature as existed at the beginning of the deinstitutionalization process suggested that those who made it outside the hospital were those who either established or otherwise fell into the care of agencies providing comprehensive 'case management' services or of compassionate individual benefactors. There seemed to be no choice: either give up the promised freedoms of deinstitutionalization in order to secure the protection of a benevolent other, or fail to cope and become a hopeless, homeless vagrant. But did people in this situation really see things in such either/or terms, or had they found other ways in which they could cope?

In both these research projects, the main question asked by the researcher was: 'What does it *feel* like to be [a modern-day Trinidad Indian; deinstitutionalized adult with mental challenges]?' This is obviously a less clear-cut question than one that could be answered with demographic statistics ('How many people were brought to Trinidad during the indenture?' 'What percentage of the modern population of Trinidad is Indian, and where on the island do they live?') or epidemiological data ('How many people are diagnosed with severe mental illness?' 'What are the main behavioral symptoms associated with mental retardation?') Answering it required the researcher to participate in the lived experience of the people under study, and not simply to observe it from a detached position.

2. Ethnographic research is used to define a problem that cannot immediately be expressed in 'If X, then Y' terms and that seems to result in behaviors that would not have been predicted by the existing literature

Standard quantitative research is predicated on the assumption that problems can best be studied if they can be stated in terms of a predictable relationship: dependent variables (factors that change) when an independent variable (a factor that seems to be a predisposing condition) is present. But sometimes, real-life problems are difficult to fit into such a testable format, at least at first.

For example, there seemed to be an unusually high rate of alcoholism among the Trinidad Indians, a fact noted with some surprise in the literature. The traditional religions of the indentured Indians (Hinduism and Islam), as well as the version of Christianity offered to them by missionaries during the colonial period, were strongly anti-drink. Why, then had the Indians – who professed to be so traditional in their cultural affiliations – become problem drinkers? There were possibly historical factors: some historians suggested that the indentured planta-tion laborers were paid in rum – a main product of the sugar estates in that era. There were also possible explanations of a psychological nature: a disenfran-chised minority tends to turn to self-destructive behaviors when its culture is threatened. There were certainly economic factors at play: poor people seek the solace of oblivion in drink or drugs in order to forget the hopelessness of their condition. But the Trinidad Indians were not disenfranchised in the same way that Native Americans, for example, had been – their alienation from the political process had for a long time been a matter of their own choice, not the result of overt discrimination. And their poverty, while marked in contrast to conditions in the First World, was not significantly worse than anyone else's in the West Indies. It was clear that the only way to sort out the apparent contradiction of Indian alco-holism was to observe it in action and to reconstruct the history of the Indians' association with alcohol as they themselves understood it.

In a similar way, the adaptation of people with *mental challenges* (particularly those with mental retardation) to life outside the hospital has been shadowed by sexual misadventure. People with mental retardation have traditionally been viewed as naïve innocents who, lacking ordinary self-control mechanisms, explode into sexual depravity at the least provocation. As such, the traditional response of caregivers has been to withhold sexual information – sexuality train-ing has rarely been part of the 'habilitation' plans along with such matters as how to make change, tell time, or read a bus schedule. But far from keeping the peo-ple in a state of innocence, such ignorance only leads to confusion, sometimes with disastrous consequences. So are people with mental retardation condemned to live as asexual beings (although physical castration or enforced sterilization is no longer a legally approved option)? Is there a way to integrate sexuality into the coping strategies of deinstitutionalized adults? Again, the answers could only come through experiencing life as the people themselves see it, not by formulat-ing judgments based on value-neutral clinical data.

3. Ethnographic research is used to identify participants in a social setting

Even when researchers set out to study a community that is considered to be well known and understood, they must realize that the dynamic of change leads to the inclusion of heretofore unacknowledged participants in the network of social interaction.

For example, the overseas Indian community was thought to revolve around the family, which, in traditional Indian culture, was a 'joint' organization (i.e. composed of a group of brothers, their wives and children sharing a common household with their father, the family patriarch). The joint family did not, as it happened, survive the indenture period. The family is still in fact central to

Indian social organization in Trinidad, but the identification of who is and is not considered 'family', and the relationships among those members, are not what they once were. Descriptive ethnography in which the contemporary family organization was 'mapped' in detail could help clarify this situation.

The situation of deinstitutionalized adults with mental retardation was also often rendered in terms of expectations and stereotypes – often depicted as dependent clients and powerful service providers and/or caregivers. This relationship is true up to a point. But for adults with mental challenges who also live in non-institutional communities, there are other elements in the social network to consider. What other people play important roles in the lives of those with mental challenges? What is the nature of their interaction? Again, detailed ethnographic description helped sort things out.

4. Ethnographic research is used to document a process

Unlike a clear-cut statistical relationship, a process is composed of numerous and ever-shifting elements. Much of life as it is really lived (as opposed to the way it can be controlled in clinical or laboratory research settings) is a matter of dynamic process.

For example, at the time of my initial field study, the main way in which the alcoholism of the Trinidad Indians was dealt with involved membership in Alcoholics Anonymous. AA has long been a reasonably successful method for helping alcoholics cope with their disease, but it was developed in the United States and grew out of a strongly Christian world-view. Why was it working among Hindu and Muslim Indians in the very different social world of Trinidad? An ethnographic study of AA in Trinidad was needed in order to document the process of recovery; how, in effect, did the Trinidad Indians take the standard elements of AA and shape them to fit their own culture and the particularities of their own situation?

The adaptation of deinstitutionalized adults to the community is clearly more than a matter of signing official release papers and sending people on their way. By following some people as they moved from custodial care to independent living, it became clear that adaptation is a complex process and one that is managed with varying degrees of success. The ability of people to hook up with formal agency supports (e.g. medical, educational, vocational, transportation, residential services) was always mediated by their ability to find informal support systems composed in various ways of peers, neighbors, family, and friends.

5. Ethnographic research is used to design setting-appropriate measures

Ethnographers are not at all opposed to the use of quantitative measures, but they do insist that such measures grow out of the local experience. While measures

24

thus modified are often based on recognized, reputable standardized tests (so that they are more useful for purposes of comparison), it is important that they be sensitive to local conditions. In some cases, such sensitivity is a matter of modifying content (e.g. some topics such as sexual behavior are freely discussed in some cultures but are taboo in others). In other cases, it may require translating the measurement instrument into language that can be understood by study participants. (Sometimes an actual other language is involved if research is being conducted in a non-English-speaking place. Or it may mean translating concepts from complex academic jargon into terms commonly used by non-scientists.) In still other cases, modification may require accommodations in the way in which the measurement instrument is administered. (For example, in some cultures, a male researcher would not be allowed to interview a female research participant, especially about personal matters, without the presence of some sort of chaperone.)

Often in quantitative research, standardized instruments are administered at the beginning of a project as they provide a lot of precise and objective data that can be used to refine working hypotheses. But in ethnographic research, the administration of such instruments is best reserved to a later part of the research process so as to give the researcher some time to learn enough about the people and their community to present the measurement instrument in ways that are considered both reasonable and acceptable.

In both the Trinidad and the deinstitutionalization research, I made use of standardized measures. In the former, I used the Health Opinion Survey (HOS), designed by medical researchers to measure levels of perceived psychosocial stress in a community. The HOS was originally used to test the correlation between stress and psychiatric disorder. I used it to see if there was a link between stress and alcoholism. The main modification was administrative. I had learned through my participant observation in the community that Indians considered alcoholism to be a social disease rather than an individual failing because they were most concerned with its negative impact on family and community relations. As such, they preferred to talk about their personal problems in groups, rather than in individual encounters. So I administered the HOS at AA meetings or social gatherings where the respondents felt free to discuss their responses with one another before marking them on the paper. This departure from accepted procedure certainly compromised the comparative value of the resulting data, but it made for unexpectedly rich results; a perspective on what people perceived to be stressful that emerged from this group discussion was far more important in this community-oriented society than the 'pure' responses of many individual respondents in a clinical setting ever could have been.

Once I had detected the concern with sexuality among deinstitutionalized people with mental challenges, I wanted to survey my population to see how much they actually knew about sex. Working with a colleague who was a psychotherapist, I came up with a diagnostic checklist that assessed both objective sexual information (e.g. anatomical details) and subjective attitudes about sexuality and relationships. Since the caregivers were in most cases very uncomfortable with discussions of this topic, it would have been disastrous to have barged in with a ready-made measurement instrument. Taking the time to develop one that reflected what I had already learned from interacting with the people (and that also relied on the trust I had established with the participants) meant that the ultimate results were meaningful to the particular people in the group I was studying. Like the Trinidad Indians, the deinstitutionalized adults found it very helpful to discuss their responses with one another; it was very important for them to have something that had the character of an ordinary conversation, rather than yet another clinical 'test' that put them as individuals on the spot.

Ethnographic methods: research settings

Ethnographic research can be done wherever people interact in 'natural' group settings. Bringing people together for a specific purpose in controlled laboratory settings is a valid technique for experimental research, but it is not ethnographic. True ethnography relies on the ability of a researcher to interact with and observe people as they essentially go about their everyday lives. As noted in Chapter 1, ethnography was developed for use in small-scale, culturally isolated communities. It later expanded for use in well-defined enclave communities (defined by race, ethnicity, age, social class, and so on) within larger societies. In our own time it has expanded still further to encompass 'communities of interest' (groups of people who share some common factor – e.g. they are all college-educated women diagnosed as HIV-positive – even if they do not regularly interact with one another) and even 'virtual communities' (formed in 'cyberspace' rather than in traditional geographic space).

===== Key points

- Ethnographic methods are of particular use when researchers need to enter a field situation in which the social issues or behaviors are not yet clearly understood.
- These methods are also worth using when getting the people's own perspective on issues is an important goal of the research.
- Specific research problems for which ethnographic methods are a useful solution include:
  - ✓ defining a research problem
  - ✓ accounting for unpredicted outcomes
  - ✓ identifying participants in a social setting
  - ✓ documenting social processes
  - ✓ designing setting-appropriate measures.

- Ethnographic research can be conducted wherever people interact in 'natural' group settings.
- Ethnographic research began in small-scale, culturally isolated communities but grew to encompass research in well-defined enclave communities within larger societies.
- Ethnographic research nowadays includes studies of 'communities of interest' and 'virtual communities' as well as traditional, geographically bounded communities.

Further reading

These books will give you more information about the studies used as examples throughout this book and about the planning and design of ethnographic research:

Angrosino, M.V. (1974) *Outside is Death: Alcoholism, Ideology, and Community Organization among the East Indians of Trinidad.* Winston-Salem, NC: Medical Behavioral Science Monograph Series.

Angrosino, M.V. (1998) *Opportunity House: Ethnographic Stories of Mental Retardation.* Walnut Creek, CA: AltaMira.

LeCompte, M.D. and Schensul, J.J. (1999) *Designing and Conducting Ethnographic Research* (Vol. I of J.J. Schensul, S. Schensul and M. LeCompte, (eds), *Ethnographer's Toolkit.* Walnut Creek, CA: AltaMira.

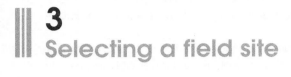

3
Selecting a field site

Chapter objectives
After reading this chapter, you should know

- the factors that must be taken into account by a researcher who is planning ethnographic research; and
- the ways in which the researcher establishes and maintains rapport so as to function as a participant observer at the field site.

In a later chapter we will take up the issues that arise with research in 'virtual' communities. But in this and the following three chapters we will be discussing what happens in the traditional (and still most common) geographically bounded field site.

Begin with a personal inventory

It is often said that the one piece of equipment that an ethnographic researcher ultimately relies on is him or herself. It is all very well to enter the field fully loaded with cameras, tape recorders, laptop computers, and so on. But in the last analysis, participant observation means that you as a researcher are interacting on a daily basis with the people being studied. It is therefore critically important for you to begin with an understanding of yourself. What kind of person are you? What types of situations do you find congenial, and which would be abhorrent? Some things are obvious: if you are highly sensitive to cold, then choosing to do fieldwork among the Inuit in northern Alaska is probably a bad idea, even if you find Inuit culture fascinating to read about. Other factors are less obvious: if you are a person who greatly values privacy, then you might do well to select a study community in which the people recognize and respect that same value. It is, of course, possible for most people to adapt to most conditions. But given the limited amount of time and financial resources that most of us have at our disposal, why not choose to do research under circumstances in which you have at least a fighting chance of fitting in? If the process of forcing yourself to adapt takes up more time and effort than the process of collecting data about the community you are studying, then participant observation is just not serving its intended purpose.

It is therefore important that you begin with a candid assessment of yourself. Check especially the following points:

- your emotional and attitudinal state;
- your physical and mental health (and the health of anyone you may be taking with you to the field);
- your areas of competence and incompetence;
- your ability to set aside preconceptions about people, behaviors, or social and political situations.

Some personal factors are under your control and you can modify them so that you can fit into a study community. Your hairstyle, choice of jewelry or bodily adornments, clothing, or tone of voice can all be adjusted if need be. On the other hand, there are things we can't do much about: our gender, our relative age, our perceived racial or ethnic category. If such distinctions are important in the study community, then you may need to think twice about inserting yourself into that culture. You may think that people in the community are wrong in their approach to gender or racial relations, but remember that your main job is that of a researcher, not a social reformer or a missionary. (Even though 'critical' ethnographers, discussed in an earlier chapter, *do* consider themselves to be social reformers, they typically become advocates for positions held by the communities with which they become identified. They do not arrive in a community with their own agenda, which they then seek to impose on the people they study.) In sum, do not choose a field site in which *you* become the object of discussion and contention.

Selecting a field site

Having subjected yourself to a thorough personal review, you can now apply more objective criteria in deciding where you want to do your research. Some of those objective criteria are scholarly in nature, others purely pragmatic. The following pointers may be useful.

1. Select a site in which the scholarly issue you are exploring is most likely to be seen in a reasonably clear fashion

You will develop a sense of the issue to be studied in a number of ways. Your research focus may be:

- a direct assignment by your instructor;
- a follow-up to a study conducted by a reputable researcher;
- an exploration of an issue that is currently in the news;
- an outgrowth of your reading of the scholarly literature – you may have identified a gap in what we think we know about a particular issue;
- the result of personal experience and your desire to gather wider information about something that affects you directly;
- an intention to work for a social or political cause by collecting information that might support that position.

Studying what happens to the traditional culture of an immigrant community such as that of the Indians of the indenture requires participant observation in an overseas Indian community that is neither too traditional nor already too assimilated. Trinidad, at the time I began my study, was just such a place.

Studying the effects of deinstitutionalization on adults with mental challenges required selecting an urban site in which such people were likely to congregate so as to find jobs, housing, and so forth. A rural community where only a single person with chronic mental illness lived, sheltered by a protective family, would not have been a reasonable choice.

2. Select a site that is comparable to others that have been studied by other researchers, but not one that has itself been over-studied

There is an ancient joke among anthropologists to the effect that the typical Navajo family consists of a mother, a father, three children, and an anthropologist. Humorous exaggeration aside, it is undeniably true that some people and places have been studied with great frequency. Communities unfortunate enough to exist in proximity to a university campus may well feel that they have been selected as research sites for their convenience almost to the point of exploitation. There is a limit to the hospitality of even the best-intentioned people. By the same token, we should not think that every research project has to begin by reinventing the wheel. Unless you have the resources to take yourself off to the highlands of New Guinea at the drop of a hat, you are most likely going to end up doing fieldwork in a community fairly close to home that has been studied before. In that case, just try to make sure that researchers are still welcome and that your own research interests are sufficiently different so that people don't feel moved to exclaim, 'Oh no! I already answered that question a dozen times!'

When I first conducted fieldwork on overseas Indians, there were a few available ethnographic reports on communities in Trinidad. But all had been conducted in isolated rural villages. I opted to base myself in a village that was still largely agrarian, but on one of the main roads with easy access to the sort of 'modern' employment (such as at a major oil refinery) that was attracting the young people of the village.

My deinstitutionalization study was inspired by research conducted in California, although I worked mainly in Florida, Tennessee, and Indiana – comparable situations, but with their own distinctive social and political attributes.

3. Select a site with a minimum of 'gatekeeping' obstacles

Routine entry requirements such as visas, vaccination certificates, or letters of introduction from local worthies usually pose no problem. But sometimes there are more troublesome matters that need to be taken care of. A background check by law enforcement officials might be necessary, particularly if you want to work in a community with a notable crime problem. Some communities that are riven by factions might require you to get permission from every conceivable interest group. Communities in authoritarian, governmentally centralized political societies might be unwilling to take the responsibility for allowing a researcher to enter without getting clearance from many levels of a bureaucratic hierarchy. Only you can decide when the process of gaining entry becomes too much of a hassle for you.

4. Select a site in which you will not be more of a burden than you are worth to the community

Remember that as a participant observer you may be living in the community you are studying; even if you are studying a place that allows you to go to your own home at the end of the day, you may be expected to be working (for pay or as a volunteer as the case may be) or in other ways drawing on the resources of the community. You will want to make sure that you can provide for your own needs as much as possible. People are often incredibly hospitable and willing to put themselves out for strangers. But keep in mind that nobody really appreciates a freeloader. *Pay particular attention to the drawing-up of a realistic budget that takes resources of both finances and time very carefully into account.* If you plan to bring your spouse and/or children to the field with you, be sure to calculate their expenses as well. If you are doing research as part of a team, consider the potential burden the community will have to bear in providing room and board to several strangers at the same time.

By the same token, make sure that you select a site in which you can adopt a role that allows for optimal participant observation. You will want to be very cautious about selecting a site in which you will be expected to be either too much of a participant or kept at arm's length.

When I first went to Trinidad to conduct research, I was a boarder in the house of a family whose oldest son had recently moved away to work in Canada. They found it pleasant to have another young man on the premises and I found it invaluable to be part of a family group – an essential prerequisite to interacting with others in an Indian cultural context. Indians are very often identified in terms of the families with which they are affiliated.

My research among deinstitutionalized adults was facilitated by my becoming a classroom volunteer at a habilitation program that served 'dually diagnosed' clients. As such, I could come and go in a natural fashion, since I had a recognized role to play; but at the same time I was not officially 'staff', so the clients felt relatively comfortable sharing their private feelings with me.

Rapport

It goes without saying that all readers of this book are wonderful, generous, outgoing, lovable people who would be welcome in communities around the world. But just in case anyone has doubts about his or her ability to fit in, a few pointers may be in order.

- *Don't assume that communities closer to home or with cultures most similar to your own will be easier to work in.* Sometimes the more you are like the people you are studying, the more they will expect of you and the less tolerant of your oddities (such as your need to collect data) they will be. It may be the case that the more of a stranger you are, the more people will be likely to help you since they will understand that you really *don't* always know what's going on.
- By the same token, don't assume that if you are working in a community very much like your own, you know everything there is to know about fitting in. *Don't take too much for granted.*
- *Do not allow yourself to be 'captured' by the first people who make you feel welcome.* It is only natural to be relieved when someone – anyone! – talks to you and seems to take an interest in your work. But it is sometimes the case that the ones who step out to do so are the community's deviants or (perhaps even worse) its self-appointed gatekeepers. Becoming too closely associated with these dubious characters may limit your opportunities to get to know everyone else.
- Therefore, *do make sure that the people who serve as your principal guides to the community are people who are themselves respected and liked.*

- *Make every effort to be helpful.* Reciprocity goes a long way toward establishing and maintaining rapport. Always be prepared to drive someone to work, baby-sit, loan someone money for groceries, and so forth. You needn't become an all-purpose servant – after all, you do have your own legitimate agenda, not to mention limitations on your own time and other resources – but don't be so wedded to your agenda that you neglect to act like a real human being interacting with other humans. Remember that some mutual obligations carry more serious implications than others: agreeing to become a baby's godparent, for example, is a matter of real gravity in some cultures, and you should carefully consider whether you are up to all the implied responsibilities before you agree. It is probably better to decline respectfully than to accept and then renege on implied promises.
- *Take the time to explain your purposes.* It is probably the case that not many people in a study community will readily understand the scholarly principles underlying your research, but just about everyone can understand your desire to collect information on issues of common concern. Most people are flattered and pleased that you are interested in them and their way of life, but if there are aspects of their way of life that they *don't* want to share, don't force them to do so. Be sure to explain as well any anticipated outcomes of your research (book, movie, museum display, website, etc.) and be forthright in discussing any possible remunerations that might be expected by members of the community.
- *Do not be afraid to express your own point of view.* You needn't become a confrontational pest, but remember that real people aren't always 'nice' – they sometimes disagree, and most people respect someone who is honest enough to have a civil discussion with them. By the same token, don't become so intent on expressing yourself that you and your opinions become the main topic of community concern.
- *Make sure that you recognize and are respectful of the social conventions that are meaningful to members of the community.* Learn what is expected of a person of your age, gender, or race and try to act accordingly. If you honestly come to feel that such expectations are degrading or otherwise emotionally unacceptable to you, the only reasonable response is to end your research and leave with a brief, polite, but clearly stated explanation.
- *Inform people about the parameters of your participant observation*: How long do you intend to stay? Do you plan to stay in touch after you leave, and if so, in what ways?
- *If you have brought your own family to the field site, make sure that all members are comfortable about interacting with their peers while you go about your own activities.*
- *If you are working as part of a research team, make sure that you do not become a clubby in-group.* Each member of the team should strive to become as much a part of the host community as feasible.

Key points

- Get to know yourself before you begin ethnographic research. What kind of person are you? What kinds of working situations do you find congenial?
- Modify aspects of personal behavior that you can control so as to conform to the norms of the study community, but be aware of local preconceptions about factors over which you have no control (e.g. gender, race, age).
- Select a research site

  ✓ in which the scholarly issues you are exploring can be seen in a reasonably clear fashion

  ✓ that is comparable with others that have been studied by researchers, but not one that has itself been over-studied

  ✓ with a minimum of gatekeeping obstacles

  ✓ in which you will not be more of a burden than you are worth to the community.

- *Establishing* and *maintaining* rapport are essential to the conduct of ethnographic research that is based on participant observation.

Further reading

The selection of field sites and the establishment of rapports are issues of these publications:

Schensul, J.J. (1999) 'Building community research partnerships in the struggle against AIDS', *Health Education and Behavior,* 26 [special issue].

Wolcott, H.F. (1994) 'The elementary school principal: notes from a field study', in H.F. Wolcott (ed.), *Transforming Qualitative Data.* Thousand Oaks, CA: Sage, pp. 103–48.

Zinn, M.B. (1979) 'Insider field research in minority communities', *Social Problems*, 27: 209–19.

4
Data collection in the field

Chapter objectives
After reading this chapter, you should know

- some of the principal data collection techniques used by ethnographic researchers who are positioned as participant observers in study communities; and
- the ways in which data collected in the field can be efficiently recorded and retrieved.

Now that we have positioned ourselves as participant observers in an ethnographic field research project, we need to consider the specific techniques that are available to us for the collection of data.

Keep in mind that participant observation is not itself a data collection technique, but rather the role adopted by an ethnographer to facilitate his or her collection of data.

It is also important to remember that good ethnography is usually the result of *triangulation* – the use of multiple data collection techniques to reinforce conclusions. (See Scrimshaw and Gleason, 1992, for a collection of articles illustrating some particular applications of the triangulation strategy; see also Flick, 2007b.)

Therefore, the following techniques may be used in combination; no one of them is by itself capable of yielding the whole picture of a living community.

'Facts' and 'reality'

Trained biologists looking at cells under a microscope can come up with accurate descriptions of the components of those cells. If they have looked at many cells over the course of time, they can determine which are the intrinsic features of a cell belonging to a certain plant or animal, and which are random deviations. Moreover, there is an assumption that any trained biologist would come to the same conclusions.

Ethnographers can rarely operate with such objective certitude. While we may strive for accuracy, we must always keep in mind that the 'facts' of human behaviors, values, and interactions are sometimes in the eye of the beholder. They can be manipulated, deliberately or otherwise, by the people being studied. The 'reality' we perceive as ethnographers is thus always conditional; we cannot take it for granted that another ethnographer, looking at the same set of 'facts' at a different time, will come to exactly the same conclusions.

Some scholars (such as the 'postmodernists' discussed earlier) would take the position that striving for 'accurate' depictions of social 'reality' through the collection of objective 'facts' is an inherently futile exercise. Statements of reality, they contend, must always be 'deconstructed' in order to discern who the observer was, and what his or her biases may have been that caused the conclusions to take the form they did. Still other scholars take the position that society is a kind of elaborate game in which observer and observed create 'reality' as they interact (much as participants in a game of football play with the objective rules of the game and so come up with a somewhat different game every time); as such their intention is not so much to characterize some sort of timeless 'reality' but to chronicle a particular snapshot of that reality. They may even be more interested in analyzing the process by which 'players' strategize their way through the 'game' than with the presumed outcome of the 'game'.

My remarks in this section are not meant to take one position or the other on these theoretical issues. I will operate on the assumption that whatever interests an ethnographer may have in analyzing his or her data, there is still the necessity to collect data in a systematic form so as to best support his or her arguments.

A note on applied ethnography

When a researcher wants to use the results of his or her fieldwork to make recommendations on public policy, or to contribute to the formation and maintenance of organizations or agencies that serve the community under study, then he or she is said to be conducting *applied ethnography* (see Chambers, 2000, for a complete review of this field). Unlike academic researchers, who can consider the 'postmodern' possibilities of ambiguity and deception raised in the previous section, applied ethnographers must proceed from a position of relative certitude. Why, after all, would anyone pay attention to their recommendations for action unless they could back up their assertions with clearly delineated, more or less objective data? So the potential for participant observation research making a real contribution to the world at large is dependent on the ethnographer being able to convince the relevant audience that he or she really does know what is going on in the study community.

In Trinidad, my research on alcoholism in the Indian community led me to rec-ommend to government health planners that public monies would be better spent on public education campaigns designed to encourage people with a problem to seek out their nearest AA group. Spending limited public monies on expensive hospital-based treatment facilities would be a waste, since most Indians would not consider anything that went on in such a setting to be legitimately therapeu-tic. The AA group, based in the kin group and the local village, was for that com-munity a more appropriate setting for recovery.

In the deinstitutionalization study, I was able to use my data to convince pro-gram managers to include sexuality training as part of the habilitation plan. I advocated against making much of the mechanics of sex (basic anatomy, etc.) since such information would likely not be absorbed by the clients. I recom-mended instead that the training focus on relationships, and suggested that 'classes' be structured not as didactic lectures but as 'role-playing' sessions in which the clients could try out styles of behavior and comment on what they had seen and participated in.

Three key skill areas

Although there are, as we shall soon see, a great many specific data collection techniques available to ethnographic researchers, all of them fit into three large categories representing the key skill areas that must be part of the repertoire of all fieldworkers: *observation, interviewing,* and *archival research.*

Observation

1. Observation is the act of perceiving the activities and interrelationships of people in the field setting through the five senses of the researcher.

Observation would seem to be the most objective of ethnographic skills, since it seems to require little or no interaction between the researcher and those he or she is studying. We must, however, remember that the objectivity of our five senses is not absolute. We all tend to perceive things through filters; sometimes these filters are an intrinsic part of the research method (e.g. our theories or analytic frameworks), but sometimes they are simply artifacts of who we are: the preconceptions that come with our social and cultural backgrounds, our genders, our relative ages, and so forth. Good ethnographers strive to be conscious of – and therefore to set aside – these latter factors, which constitute a perspective we call *ethnocentrism* (the assumption – conscious or otherwise – that our own way of thinking about and doing things is somehow more natural and preferable to all others). But we can never banish them completely.

In the ideal, observation begins the moment the researcher enters the field setting, where he or she will strive to set aside all preconceptions and take nothing for granted. It is sometimes said that the ethnographer becomes like a little child, to whom everything in the world is new. As a result, the process of observation begins by taking everything in and recording it in as much detail as possible, with as little interpretation as possible. (For example, one might observe, 'The people at the temple were chanting and swaying to the beat of a drum' rather than 'The people at the temple were carried away by religious ecstasy.') Gradually, as the researcher gains more experience in the field site, he or she can begin to discern matters that seem to be important and to concentrate on them, while paying proportionately less attention to things that are of lesser significance. It is vital to the outcome of the research that the ethnographer also come to recognize *patterns* – behaviors or actions that seem to be repeated so that they can be said to be typical of the people being studied (as opposed to unique and perhaps random occurrences).

We may think we all have a natural facility for observing and describing the people and events that surround us. But in fact, what we usually have is a well-developed screening process. When we are functioning in our own everyday worlds, it would simply be inefficient if we paid complete and objective attention to everything, even things very familiar to us. In our own worlds, we learn to focus. That which we do not 'see' is almost always greater than that which we do. Notwithstanding the weight we grant to 'eyewitness' accounts, the fact is eyewitnesses can be quite unreliable because most of us have gotten used to tuning out most descriptors. So ethnographic observation cannot depend solely on our 'natural' facilities. We have to work hard to really and truly see all the many details of a new situation – or (as in the case of the deinstitutionalization study) to see familiar situations through the eyes of those who are in many ways 'strangers' to those situations.

Some observational techniques are said to be *unobtrusive*, which has traditionally meant that those under study do not know that they are being observed. Modern standards of ethical research, which include procedures for 'informed consent' (which will be discussed in a later chapter), have greatly restricted the scope of truly unobtrusive observation. It is still possible, however, to observe people in public places where you as a researcher can just blend in (e.g. making notes about how people seat themselves in an airport waiting room or a Department of Motor Vehicles office); it is not necessary to explain oneself or obtain permission from people so observed. The study of such spatial relationships is known as *proxemics*; the related study of people's 'body language' is technically known as *kinesics* (see Bernard, 1988, pp. 290–316 for an extended discussion of unobtrusive techniques). Researchers must, however, be sensitive to matters of privacy even in 'public' spaces. It is not likely that anything very intimate will happen in an airport waiting area. But conducting proxemic observations in a public restroom might certainly be questionable.

Careful, reasonably unobtrusive observations of proxemic and kinesic behavior can tell us a great deal about the unspoken assumptions of cultures. Among the Trinidad Indians, there is a restricted sense of private space as compared with North Americans. Houses of the more tradition-minded people often lack doors or other partitions demarcating sleeping areas from other living areas. On the other hand, the people are quite distant and reserved in terms of interpersonal space: there is very little hugging, hand-holding, or other forms of emotional expression, at least in public places. Keeping 'good posture' seems to be important and children are sometimes explicitly reprimanded for 'slouching around'. A rather formal conversational distance is maintained in most circumstances. Indians sometimes express disdain for non-Indian Trinidadians who, they say, 'are all over you all the time'.

Adults with mental retardation often have not mastered the nuances of expected proxemic and kinesic behavior typical of the mainstream in the United States. Indeed, among the most important cues marking people as 'retarded' are those having to do with improper use of spatial and body language. People with mental retardation tend to be very vigorous touchers and huggers – they often seem to 'invade the space' of others. On the other hand, they seem to have a paradoxically highly developed sense of their own personal space. If one of the men in the program had his own room – or even his side of a shared room – he would defend it passionately and sometimes fly into a rage if anyone came into it without being explicitly invited.

There are other kinds of unobtrusive research that are still ethically defensible. For example, *behavior trace studies* are very much like archeological excavations, but among the living. There has been much publicity about 'garbology' projects – research based on sifting through people's trash in order to find clues about how they live. One might question how truly 'unobtrusive' such a project could be (I, for one, would definitely notice teams of researchers picking through my garbage and perhaps even give some second thoughts to what I am throwing away), but even if the subject knows that he or she is being studied and gives permission for researchers to proceed, there need be no further interaction between researchers and subjects.

Given the ethical concerns about absolutely 'unobtrusive' observation (as even the most innocuous project could be considered 'deceptive' under some circumstances), ethnographers rely much more frequently on observations of settings in which they are known to the participants and in which they may well be engaged in the activities themselves (*participant observation*). But just because the behavior of people in a research setting unfolds in a seemingly haphazard fashion (or so it may seem to the 'little child' researcher at the beginning of a field study), this does not mean that the observational process itself should be haphazard. Good ethnographic observation necessarily involves some degree of structure. At minimum, researchers should cultivate the habit of taking well-organized field notes that include:

- a statement about the particular setting (e.g. school, home, church, store);
- an enumeration of the participants (number, general characteristics, e.g. ages, genders);
- descriptions of the participants (rendered in as nearly objective a form as possible: 'The man wore a torn, dirty pair of pants', not 'The man looked poor');
- chronology of events;
- descriptions of the physical setting and all material objects involved (in great detail, taking nothing for granted);
- descriptions of behaviors and interactions (avoiding interpretations: 'The man was weeping and repeatedly struck his head with his fist', not 'The man looked deranged' – particularly if video recording equipment is not possible);
- records of conversations or other verbal interactions (as near to verbatim as possible, particularly if it is not feasible or desirable to have a tape recorder running).

Some projects involving multiple members in a team approach rely on finely tuned and standardized note-taking processes. But even if you are on your own, you should train yourself to be as meticulous as possible in recording data. The more nearly your records of observations at selected sites contain the same information, the more efficient it will be to retrieve and compare data.

My research on alcoholism as a factor in the lives of modern Trinidad Indians led me to numerous observations at meetings of Alcoholics Anonymous, which had been imported to the island from the United States in the 1960s. Keeping structured notes enabled me to readily answer such questions as: What is the average age of the 'recovering' Trinidad Indian alcoholic? (45–50 years). Is there a particular order of speakers? (yes, those only briefly sober speak first, building up to those with many years of documented sobriety whose 'witness' is therefore surrounded by greater solemnity). Are Indians the island's only alcoholics? (no, but they are – with extremely rare exceptions – the only ones who attend AA meetings). What is the role of women? (they provide refreshments, but do not speak). I was not, strictly speaking, a 'participant' observer at AA meetings since I am not a recovering alcoholic. But I was brought to my first meetings by informants who did fit that category, and who introduced me to the membership at large. After a while my presence became an accepted thing.

I spent several years as a participant observer (as a volunteer tutor) in classrooms where adults with mental retardation were being taught basic skills. Since I was 'participating', I had less opportunity to make detailed notes while on site, and therefore had to cultivate the skill of reconstructing my observations as soon as possible thereafter. The keeping of structured notes was especially helpful when I began observing other programs in my own area (e.g. those that served only people with mental retardation as opposed to the program that dealt with 'dually diagnosed' clients) and programs in other states where somewhat different laws and standards of care were in operation. The structured observations in all these settings made it possible to compare and contrast behaviors and interactions that seemed to be dependent on factors beyond the clients' control, such as the requirements of various bureaucratic systems (e.g. criminal justice, education).

A note on notes

The importance of keeping structured and organized field notes when conducting observational research cannot be overemphasized, whether one is doing the research solo or as part of a team. It is worth keeping in mind the following points about maintaining field notes:

- Make sure that every note 'card' (or whatever format you find most congenial for recording) is headed by the date, place, and time of observation.
- Be sure to record as many verbatim verbal exchanges as possible; nothing conveys the sense of 'being there' more than the actual words of the participants.
- Use pseudonyms or other codes to identify participants in order to preserve anonymity and confidentiality – you never know when unauthorized people might try to sneak a peek. One piece of advice from bitter personal experience: don't make your code system so complex and obscure that even you can't reconstruct the cast of characters.
- Be sure to record events in sequence; some researchers find it helpful to divide their notepad (the same advice goes for those who take notes directly onto laptop computers) into hours or even minutes so that they can precisely place actions in order.
- Keep all descriptions of people and material objects on an objective level; try to avoid making inferences based solely on appearances (See Adler and Adler, 1994, and Angrosino and Mays de Pérez, 2000, for more comprehensive reviews of the theory, methods, and ethical ramifications of observational research.)

Interviewing

> 2. Interviewing is a process of directing a conversation so as to collect information.

The hallmark of observational research, as noted several times in the previous section, is to record details in as nearly objective a descriptive manner as possible, avoiding interpretations and inferences, and setting aside one's own preconceptions. The ethnographer ultimately comes to a point of recognizing or inferring meaningful patterns in observed behaviors. But the inevitable next question is: what, exactly, *do* those behaviors mean? At that point, it is necessary to start asking questions of knowledgeable people in the community or group under study. Interviewing thus grows logically out of observation.

We have noted that while observation seems to be nothing more than what we do in everyday life, it really requires a heightened degree of consciousness, awareness of fine-grained detail, and the careful recording of structured, organized data in order for it to be useful as a research tool. In a similar fashion, we might be tempted to think that interviewing, which is a kind of conversation after all, is something we can all do. Moreover, we see 'interviews' all the time on TV – it all looks so effortless. Why, then, would anyone call the sort of in-depth, open-ended interviewing typical of ethnographic research 'the most technically challenging and, at the same time, the most innovative and exciting form' of data collection? (This is a position taken by Stephen Schensul, Jean Schensul, and Margaret LeCompte in the comprehensive, multi-volume, widely used *Ethnographer's Toolkit*.) It is clear that there is more to ethnographic interviewing than having an ordinary conversation such as you would have with a friend; it is also different in some way from the sort of TV interview in which both interviewer and celebrity subject are more or less following a predetermined script and have tailored their remarks to fit a limited time frame.

Ethnographic interviewing is indeed conversational in the sense that it takes place between people who have grown to be friends as the ethnographer has been a participant observer in the community in which his or her respondent lives. In that sense, it is different from the kind of interviewing that might be done by a news reporter prying information from a 'source'. It is certainly not the same as a police officer grilling a suspect or a lawyer interrogating a witness or a health care professional taking a medical history from a patient. But on the other hand, it must necessarily go beyond the parameters of an ordinary friendly conversation, since the researcher does need to find out certain things and must be vigilant in keeping the conversation on track – all without seeming to be coercive or impatient.

The ethnographic interview is therefore typically *open-ended* in nature – it flows conversationally and accommodates digressions, which may well open up new avenues of inquiry that the researcher had not originally considered. In that sense it is a kind of partnership in which the informed insider helps the researcher develop the inquiry as it goes along.

The ethnographic interview is also conducted *in depth*. It is not merely an oral version of a shotgun survey questionnaire. Instead, it is intended to probe for meaning, to explore nuances, to capture the gray areas that might be missed in either/or questions that merely suggest the surface of an issue.

In order to make an interview work for maximal ethnographic results, the interviewer should prepare by reviewing everything he or she already knows about the topic at hand and coming up with some general questions that he or she wants to know more about. These questions should not harden into a checklist of survey items, but should serve as a guide for the main points of the conversation. Although the interview may be unstructured (in the sense of not being tethered to a formal set of survey questions), it is by no means haphazard. In addition to the open-ended questions with which the interviewer enters the encounter, there will be a variety of *probe questions* designed to keep the interview moving in productive directions. Some examples of useful probes include:

- neutral acknowledgements ('Yes, I see … ');
- repeating what the person has said as a question to make sure that you have understood correctly ('So your family built the house on that side of the village in order to be nearer to the shrine?');
- asking for more information ('Why did your older brother think he needed to go to England for further study?');
- asking for clarification of apparent contradictions ('You told me you were born in 1925 but you described the arrival of the last indenture ship [which was in 1917] … ');
- asking for an opinion ('You described your teenage daughter going out on dates. What do you think of the way young people act nowadays?');
- asking for clarification of a term ('You talk about "liming" along the road. What, exactly, does that mean?' [idling with a gang of friends, usually with alcohol involved]), or a complex process ('Please take me one more time through the steps in refining sugar cane into molasses');
- asking for lists of things in order to get a better sense of how insiders categorize and organize the world around them ('What kinds of beverages besides rum do they sell in a "rum shop"?');
- requesting *narratives of experience* – concrete anecdotes that illustrate a general point ('You speak of boys being "led astray" by drink. Can you tell me about a particular time when *you* felt you were "led astray"?').

Complementing these positive steps that you can take to make an interview work, there are several things to avoid – things that might add up to *interviewer bias*. For example, *do not*:

- ask leading questions ('Aren't you ashamed of all the bad things you did when you were drinking heavily?');
- ignore leads when the interviewee introduces new themes that seem important to him or her;
- redirect or interrupt a story;
- ignore the interviewee's non-verbal cues (e.g. signs of boredom or anger);
- ask questions that seem to tell the interviewee the answer you want ('Don't you agree that AA has accomplished a great deal for the benefit of alcoholics in Trinidad?');
- use non-verbal cues (e.g. vigorous nodding of the head, leaning over to shake the interviewee's hand) to indicate when the interviewee has given you the 'right' answer.

In addition to these specific techniques designed to keep the interview flowing, there are several points that speak to the overall 'etiquette' of conducting an interview:

- Try to avoid interjecting yourself too much into the narrative. Some manuals advise against ever expressing your own opinions, but I would not go so far – you are, after all, a real person with your own perspective, and you will not likely impress the person you are talking to if you act like a blank wall. But neither should you use the interview as a forum for expounding your own ideas or criticizing or belittling the ideas of the person you are interviewing.
- Maintain good eye contact. This does not mean staring fixedly at the person you are interviewing – doing so would probably only convince the interviewee that you are a lunatic. 'Normal' eye contact involves occasionally glancing away. But it certainly does not include prolonged periods of staring off into space, minutely examining your tape recorder, intently writing notes, or fiddling with your computer.
- Try to monitor and avoid undesirable non-verbal cues (e.g. facial gestures that indicate disgust or disapproval, moving your chair away from that of the person you are talking to).
- Spend some time in ice-breaking chit-chat. Plunging directly into the interview tends to give the session a police-grilling quality. Allow for some getting-to-know-you time (which may be shorter or longer depending on the mood of the person you are interviewing or the amount of time you have allotted for the session) even if it appears that the topic of such 'small talk' is somewhat off track. In fact, in participant observation research, nothing is ever really completely off track – important proxemic and kinesic cues, as well as clues about people's values and attitudes, often come through in these unguarded conversational moments. So even if the conversation appears casual, you cannot be completely 'off duty'.

- Accept hospitality when offered. Many ethnographic interviews are held in homes, restaurants, or other places where people normally meet to talk (i.e. not sterile labs, imposing offices, or hushed libraries) and it is only natural to share some refreshment as long as it comes in the form of manageable snacks – if a large, elaborate meal is in the offing, it is better to postpone the interview.
- Be aware of the condition of the person you are interviewing; do not overtax those who are in frail health or otherwise distracted, no matter how much you would like to adhere to your own agenda.
- *Do your homework!* While you may not yet have developed your own in-depth understanding of the people and their way of life when you begin your interviews, you should at that point not be completely in the dark. There will be things you have observed that you want to ask about – events, behaviors, expressed points of view that you will want to pursue and clarify. By this point you should know something about the major social institutions in the community, as well as something about the history of the group. You should also have at least a rough idea of who is who in the community and how they relate to one another.
- Personalize the interview. Ask the person you are talking to to share photos, scrapbooks, and other memorabilia that lend a personal touch to the commentary. You may also want to ask the interviewee's permission to borrow those materials to copy or study further. If so, the originals should always be returned promptly and in the same condition as you received them. (If these items are of particular historical or cultural value, you may want to discuss with the interviewee the possibility of donating them to a museum, library, or other appropriate public institution.)

Some specialized interview types

The general instructions for the ethnographic interview as outlined above will serve well in most cases, but there are some situations in which specialized variants on the interview method are helpful.

The *genealogical interview* was a staple of traditional anthropologists (and other social scientists interested in the lives of people in non-urban settings) because kinship – the ties of family and marriage – were often central to the ways in which 'pre-modern' communities were organized. The systematic collection of genealogical data could be used to elicit information about the patterns of interpersonal relations in the community. It could also be applied to studies of rules of descent (including ownership of property), marriage, and residence, as well as to studies of migration patterns and religious practices.

Kinship is rarely as central to modern urban communities as it was in the small-scale folk societies of earlier times. But even with increased mobility, the 'ties that bind' are merely attenuated, not absent. 'Blood' and marriage may no longer define a person's place in the world, but the ways in which people establish and maintain relationships with one another are still governed by definable patterns and expectations – they are not random or disorganized. And so the traditional genealogical method has evolved into the *social network analysis*, which traces the connections among people in extended situations (such as members of the geographically widely dispersed Indian 'diaspora'), often relying on sophisticated computer models to sort out these widely ramified links. Although in such cases the analysis per se needs to be done by complex technology, the data are initially generated by the same old-fashioned ethnographic means – asking people questions about their relationships – that characterized the genealogical studies of several decades ago.

Using genealogical interviewing methods, I was able to determine that the pattern of sponsorship in the Trinidad AA operated through kinship lines. A man's drinking partners were likely to be close relatives (especially his cousins on his father's side) and when any one of them decided to seek sobriety, he would sponsor other members of the group. It happened that many of the regional AA groups were in fact composed of the members of what had once been a kin-based 'drinking crew'.

It was very difficult to elicit genealogical information from the adults with mental retardation, but from what I was able to glean I was able to see that those who recognized a strong kin network were usually more successful in completing their training than those who felt disconnected from even abandoned by their relatives. While not conclusive by any means, such an insight could form the basis for a more structured survey that could at a later date either confirm or disprove the association between strength of family ties and successful completion of a habilitation program.

Oral history is a field of study dedicated to the reconstruction of the past through the experiences of those who have lived it. While those with political or economic power often write their memoirs of great events, the ordinary people have often not had the opportunity to tell their stories. Oral history therefore provides a way for those previously marginalized and rendered voiceless (e.g. women, members of minority groups, the poor, people with disabilities or of alternate sexual orientation) to put their stories on the record. The oral history interviewer brings together as many of the surviving participants in a given event of some significance (be it local, regional, national, or international) and gives them the opportunity to tell their personal stories – all of which together form a mosaic representation of that event. That representation may give us a different picture from that enshrined in the official history books and thus help put that official picture into a larger perspective.

A variant of oral history interview is the form of research known as the *life-history*. Rather than aim at a composite reconstruction of a particular event as in oral history, life history attempts to see the past through the microcosm of the life of one particular individual. Depending on the theoretical predisposition of the researcher, that individual could either be a 'typical' or 'representative' member of his or her community (such that his or her life story stands in for all those whose stories are not recorded) or an 'extraordinary' person (who represents the values and aspirations of the group).

The analysis of the extended narratives generated by oral and life-history research has been aided considerably by the development of computer software designed to pull out themes and patterns. But as in social network studies, no matter how sophisticated the technology of analysis has become, the generation of data remains at heart the product of a traditional ethnographic interview.

My understanding of how and why the Trinidad Indians had become alcoholic despite a heritage of anti-alcohol culture was shaped by the oral history I collected from men who were in their forties and fifties at the time of my original research. They remembered back to the days of the second World War when Trinidad was used as a base by the U.S. air force. Trinidad was not in the thick of the war, and the young airmen had a lot of time on their hands – time they used by succumbing to the sensual pleasures of a tropical island. It was they who introduced the strongly American-influenced 'rum and Coca Cola' culture of conspicuous consumption and hedonism. The young Indian men of that generation saw that the old colonial plantation system was a dead end, and they eagerly sought the jobs provided at the air base. But along with the jobs came the lifestyle they saw among the Americans. Drinking was no longer a taboo – it became part and parcel of the young Indians' embrace of new economic potentialities.

Life histories form the basis of my research into the experiences of deinstitutionalized adults with mental retardation. Since my aim was to understand what it feels like to be mentally challenged in a complex, high-tech world, I could do no better than to see how people diagnosed with that condition had confronted the challenges of life. Unlike a clinical interview, which would focus on the specifics of the handicapping condition, a life-history interview gave the respondents the opportunity to talk about what was important to *them* in the course of their lived experiences. It was thus that I was able to discover the very strong concern about sexuality and the development of truly adult relationships.

While the classic ethnographic interview is open-ended in nature, as described above, it is also possible to conduct *semi-structured interviews*, which use predetermined questions related to 'domains of interest' (e.g. 'What are the ways people earn a living in this village?', 'What types of community-based programs are available to deinstitutionalized adults with mental retardation?'). Unlike the open-ended interview, which can roam rather freely around the area delineated by the general research questions, the semi-structured interview sticks closely to the prearranged topic and features questions designed to elicit information specifically about that topic. Digressions and new directions, so important in the open-ended interview, are not part of the semi-structured interview plan. The semi-structured interview should naturally develop out of an open-ended interview, following up and clarifying issues that came up in the course of the earlier, more conversational format.

The semi-structured interview may also be used to operationalize general factors into measurable variables, which can then be developed into working hypotheses, which in turn form the basis for a formal *ethnographic survey* (a closed-ended instrument designed to collect quantitative data from a relatively large number of informants). The mechanics of quantitative research are treated in the books by Flick (2007a, 2007b) in this series. The important point to keep in mind here is that in ethnographic research the large-scale survey with hypotheses testable through quantified data is an *outgrowth* of prior open-ended observations and interviews; it is not a stand-alone method. Its strength is dependent on the value of the qualitative data that inform it (see Kvale, 2007, for more details of doing interviews).

A note on sampling

While there are recognized canons for determining the size of a population to be sampled in a purely quantitative study, the question of 'How many [people should I interview, events should I observe]?' can become something of a problem in ethnographic research. The best answer – although not necessarily the neatest or most definitive one – is that

> the size of a sample depends on the characteristics of the group you are studying, on your own resources (i.e. legitimate limitations on your time, mobility, access to equipment, and so forth), and on the objectives of your study.

As general as that rule may be, there are a few specific points you may wish to consider. Your sample should reflect the heterogeneity of the group you are studying. If it is a very diverse population, then you will need to interview and observe more in order to be sure that you have a good overview of all the different elements within the group. In a purely homogeneous group, a single person case study would be a legitimate 'sample'. But as most study communities are in fact diverse to one degree or another, you should be aware of the range of variation and include interviews and observations that reflect that range.

A note on recording interview data

Interview data are typically recorded on audiotape. Taping is a way of assuring the accuracy of what is said and, in the case of oral/life histories, it is essential to have the actual spoken voice available for replay. It should be noted, however, that audiotaping requires a fair amount of equipment (a recorder, possibly an external microphone, blank tapes, working batteries or an available electric outlet) that may not always be feasible to acquire and tote around. While it is possible nowadays to buy reasonably inexpensive, more or less unobtrusive, but good-quality audiotape equipment, the cost of equipment goes up when one needs higher quality (e.g. for recording those voices that in and of themselves need to be preserved for posterity). Moreover, recorded tapes are only the beginning of a process; tapes need to be indexed and, in most cases, transcribed so that information can be efficiently retrieved from them. At best transcription is a slow, tedious process and the average researcher will have neither the time nor the skill to do it properly. On the other hand, the services of a professional transcriber can price a project out of the ballpark.

Although more and more ethnographers are using videotape to record a variety of social interactions, it has not become a standard way of recording interviews, except among those who plan to use their interviews as part of filmed documentaries or other visual reports, or those who are particularly interested in capturing and analyzing the non-verbal aspects of the conversation. Although videotape equipment is readily available and not necessarily very expensive, it makes the transcription process even more difficult than is the case with audiotape. Moreover, videotaped interviews present serious problems when maintaining the confidentiality of participants is at issue.

Unless one is an expert stenographer – and such people are becoming rare to the point of extinction – it is usually impossible to keep an accurate written record of an interview. Even if one were such an expert, it would be inadvisable to rely on such a technique as the researcher would then be spending an inordinate amount of time looking at his or her notepad, and thus losing valuable eye contact with the person being interviewed. An occasional jotted note is fine, but a complete written record is neither feasible nor desirable for most ethnographic interviews.

So, for better or worse, the audiotape remains the most valuable adjunct to the conduct of interviews and to the subsequent retrieval and analysis of the interview data. (See Schensul et al., 1999, pp. 121–200, for a thorough exposition of the theory and method of ethnographic interviewing.)

Archival research

> 3. Archival research is the analysis of materials that have been stored for research, service, and other purposes both official and unofficial.

Individuals and groups tend to collect stuff relevant to their histories, achievements, and future plans. Sometimes the stuff is highly organized (e.g. minutes of meetings of a board of directors, family photo albums lovingly maintained by an ardent genealogist, back issues of newspapers). But more often than not it is simply stored rather haphazardly and is thus often in a poor state of preservation. The challenge to the ethnographer is to find such sources of information, to make sense of them (in the likely event that they are not already organized), and to assist in their preservation for future researchers.

Some archived materials were originally collected for bureaucratic or administrative purposes. These are known as *primary sources* and may include:

- maps
- records of births, deaths, marriages, real estate transactions
- census, tax, and voting rolls
- specialized surveys
- service system records from human service organizations
- court proceedings
- minutes of meetings.

It should be noted that even if these materials are highly organized and in a good state of preservation, they were not likely collected for the same purposes that animate the researcher. So the latter must still sort through them to get them to tell the story that he or she needs to hear.

Another potentially important form of archival data are the *secondary data* resulting from another researcher's study. For example, a colleague who did fieldwork in Trinidad the year before I arrived had collected a great deal of genealogical information in support of her study of the transmission of certain genetic illnesses. I was not interested in genetics, but I was able to use the data she graciously loaned me to support my growing suspicion about the link between kinship ties and AA sponsorship. The fruits of many research projects are now available in excerpted and catalogued form on computerized databases. The Human Relations Area File is perhaps the best known of these sources of cross-cultural information.

Archival research rarely stands alone as an ethnographic skill, although it can certainly be the basis of a respectable stand-alone study if first-hand fieldwork is not feasible. But accessing and interpreting archived materials is almost always facilitated when the researcher does have first-hand experience in the community under study, and when he or she can check inferences made from the archived data in interviews with living members of the community under study.

There are several advantages to archival research:

- It is generally non-reactive. The researcher does not influence people's responses, since he or she is not interacting directly with the people who provided the information.
- It is usually relatively inexpensive.
- It is particularly important when one is interested in studying changing events or behaviors through time.
- It is also valuable when studying topics that might be considered too sensitive or volatile to observe or ask questions about directly.

On the other hand, the ethnographer using archived material should be aware of some potential problems.

- Archived data are not always unbiased: Who collected it? For what purposes? What might have been left out (intentionally or otherwise) in the collection process? Even haphazard collection results from a process of editorial selection; the researcher who comes along later is therefore not dealing with 'pure' information.
- Even modern computerized databases are not always free of error: just because the information has been carefully transcribed does not mean that it was accurate to begin with.
- There can be physical or logistical problems in working with these data, which may be stored in inconvenient or physically unattractive (dusty, dirty, rat- or roach-infested) places.

Despite these caveats, however, archived data are simply too rich a resource to be ignored. (Berg, 2004, pp. 209–32, provides an excellent overview of the use of archival materials in ethnographic research.)

In sum, good ethnographic research relies on a composite of observational, interview, and archival sources.

Key points

- Good ethnography is the result of triangulation – the use of multiple data collection techniques to reinforce conclusions.
- Ethnographic data collection techniques fall into three main skill areas:
  - ✓ observation
  - ✓ interviewing
  - ✓ analysis of archival materials.
- Observation is the act of perceiving the activities and interrelationships of people in the field setting through the five senses of the researcher. It requires
  - ✓ objective recording
  - ✓ a search for patterns.
- Observational techniques may be
  - ✓ unobtrusive (e.g. proxemics, kinesics, behavior trace studies)
  - ✓ participant-based.
- Interviewing is a process of directing a conversation so as to collect information. There are several types of interview used by ethnographers:

✓ open-ended, in-depth
✓ semi-structured (contribute to quantitative survey research)
✓ specialized types:

  ➢ genealogical and network analysis interviews
  ➢ oral and life histories.

• Archival research is the analysis of materials that have been stored for research, service, and other purposes both official and unofficial. There are both primary and secondary sources of archival data.

Further reading

These resources will give you more information about the key methods presented in this chapter:

Adler, P.A. and Adler, P. (1994) 'Observational techniques', in N.K. Denzin and Y.S. Lincoln (eds), *Handbook of Qualitative Research* (2nd ed.). Thousand Oaks, CA: Sage, pp. 377–92.

Angrosino, M.V. and A. Mays de Pérez (2000) 'Rethinking observation: from method to context', in N.K. Denzin and Y.S. Lincoln (eds), *Handbook of Qualitative Research* (2nd ed.). Thousand Oaks, CA: Sage, pp. 673–702.

Flick, U. (2007a) *Designing Qualitative Research* (Book 1 of *The SAGE Qualitative Research Kit*). London: Sage.

Kvale, S. (2007) *Doing Interviews* (Book 2 of *The SAGE Qualitative Research Kit*). London: Sage.

Schensul, S.L., Schensul, J.J. and LeCompte, M.D. (1999) *Essential Ethnographic Methods: Observations, Interviews, and Questionnaires* (Vol. II of J.J. Schensul, S.L. Schensul and M. LeCompte, (eds), *Ethnographer's Toolkit*). Walnut Creek, CA: AltaMira.

5
Focus on observation

Chapter objectives
After reading this chapter, you should

- know more about the concepts and procedures associated with the technique of observation; and thus
- understand better one of the three main ethnographic operations discussed in the previous chapter.

A definition of observation

We have seen that ethnographic research is a judicious mix of observation, interviewing, and archival study. Since other volumes in this series will treat the latter two in some detail (see Kvale, 2007; Rapley, 2007), we will take a closer look at *observation* here, both in its participant and non-participant aspects.

The key role of observation in social research has long been acknowledged. Indeed, our human ability to observe the world around us forms the basis for our ability to make commonsense judgments about things. Much of what we know about our surroundings comes from a lifetime of observation. However, observation in the research content is considerably more systematic and formal a process than the observation that characterizes everyday life. Ethnographic research is predicated on the regular and repeated observation of people and situations, often with the intention of responding to some theoretical question about the nature of behavior or social organization.

A simple dictionary definition may serve to help us situate observation as a tool of research. That is:

Observation is the act of noting a phenomenon, often with instruments, and recording it for scientific purposes.

Implicit in this definition is the fact that when we make note of something, we do so using all of our senses. In everyday usage, we often restrict observation to the visual, but a good ethnographer must be aware of information coming in from all sources.

Types of observational research

Although in its earliest manifestations as a research tool observation was supposed to be 'non-reactive', in fact observation presupposes some sort of contact with the people or things being observed. Ethnographic observation (as opposed to the sort of observation that might be conducted in a clinical setting) is conducted in the field, in naturalistic settings. The observer is thus, to one degree or another, involved in that which he or she is observing.

This question of degree speaks to the kind of *role* adopted by the ethnographer. The classic typology of researcher roles is that of Gold (1958), who distinguished four categories:

- In the *complete observer* role, the ethnographer is as detached as possible from the setting under study. Observers are neither seen nor noticed. Such a role was thought to represent a kind of ideal of objectivity, although it is pretty much out of favor because it can lend itself to deception and raise ethical issues that contemporary researchers try to avoid. Nevertheless, some interesting and valid examples of the genre continue to appear, such as Cahill's (1985) study of interaction order in a public bathroom. This study was concerned with routine bathroom behavior. Over a nine-month period, Cahill and five student assistants observed behavior in the bathrooms of shopping malls, student centers on college campuses, and restaurants and bars.
- The *observer-as-participant* role finds the researcher conducting observations for brief periods, perhaps in order to set the context for interviews or other types of research. The researcher is known and recognized, but relates to the 'subjects' of study solely *as* a researcher. For example, Fox (2001) conducted observations in a prison-based group designed to encourage

'cognitive self-change' among violent offenders. Fox's research purposes were explained to and endorsed by the state Department of Corrections, as well as by the facilitators and members of the group. 'Although I interact with other participants,' she says, 'most of the time I take notes quietly.'

- The researcher who is a *participant-as-observer* is more fully integrated into the life of the group under study and is more engaged with the people; he or she is as much a friend as a neutral researcher. His or her activities as a researcher are still acknowledged, however. For example, Anderson (1990) and his wife spent fourteen summers living in two adjacent communities, one black and low-income, the other racially mixed but becoming increasingly middle-to-upper income and white. During this time he developed a study of interactions involving young black men on the streets of the two communities. Those young men were aware of the stereotype evoked by their status, and resented the way they were treated (i.e. avoided) by others who assumed they were dangerous; but they were also able to play up that presumed character in order to achieve certain advantages in some circumstances.

- When the researcher is a *complete participant*, however, he or she disappears completely into the setting and is fully engaged with the people and their activities, perhaps even to the extent of never acknowledging his or her own research agenda. In traditional anthropological parlance, this stance was somewhat disparagingly referred to as 'going native'. On the other hand, there is considerable support for the development of 'indigenous fieldwork', that is, research conducted by people who are members of the culture they study (da Matta, 1994, has discussed this matter in some detail). It is sometimes assumed that a 'native' of the culture will achieve greater rapport with the people being observed, although that is not necessarily the case, as sometimes 'blending in' totally fatally compromises the ability of the researcher to conduct the research. It is an interesting paradox that at both ends of the continuum – whether the researcher is fully engaged in or completely detached from the setting – ethical problems related to deceptive practices may arise. As a result, most ethnographers position themselves somewhere within the second two roles.

Given the focus on those two forms of engagement, it is not surprising that analysts now tend to discuss roles in terms of *membership* (see, e.g., Adler and Adler, 1994):

- Researchers who adopt *peripheral* membership observe and interact closely with the people under study, and thereby establish identities as insiders, but they do not participate in those activities constituting the core of group membership. For example, researchers studying drug culture on the streets of a big city would need to establish themselves as people who are known and can be trusted, even though it is understood that they will not use or sell drugs themselves (see, e.g., Bourgois, 1995).

55

- By contrast, those who adopt an *active* membership role do engage in those core activities, although they try to refrain from committing themselves to the group's values, goals, and attitudes. For example, the anthropologist Christopher Toumey (1994) studied a group of creationists; he participated fully in their meetings and socialized freely with them at their homes, although he made it clear that as an anthropologist he could not agree with their philosophical position on the theory of evolution.
- Researchers who take on *complete* membership, however, study settings in which they are active and engaged members. They are also often advocates for the positions adopted by the group. For example, Ken Plummer (2005) discusses the ways in which he came out as a gay man, became involved with a political movement to reform laws about homosexuality in his native Britain, and began to study the gay scene in London in the late 1960s.

Ethnographic research in which the researcher adopts one of these membership roles may be termed *participant observation*, which is a 'process of learning through exposure to or involvement in the day-to-day or routine activities of participants in the research setting' (Schensul et al., 1999, p. 91). We should not, however, think of participant observation as a research method; it is, rather, a 'strategy that facilitates data collection in the field' (Bernard, 1988, p. 150). The term is a combination of the role of the researcher (participant of some sort) with an actual data collection technique (observation). Researchers may, of course, use other data collection techniques (surveys, archival searches, interviews) while they are participants in the community under study; but the assumption is that even as they do these other things, they are still being careful observers of the people and events around them.

The task of observational research

Observational techniques are suitable for research dealing with

- *specific settings* (e.g. a shopping mall, a church, a school);
- *events*, which are defined as sequences of activities longer and more complex than single actions; they usually take place in a specific location, have a defined purpose and meaning, involve more than one person, have a recognized history, and are repeated with some regularity; a Presidential election in the United States is an example of an 'event' in this sense;
- *demographic factors* (e.g. indicators of socioeconomic differences, such as types of housing/building materials, presence of indoor plumbing, presence and number of intact windows, method of garbage disposal, legal or illegal sources of electrical power).

In order to function as an observer – even one with relatively minimal interaction with the population being studied – it is necessary to have the following qualities:

- *language skills* (an obvious prerequisite when conducting research in a place where your own language is not the one used by the people being studied, but also true even when everyone speaks the same language in the technical sense, but different groups have their own in-group slang or jargon or attach different meanings to the language of gesture and posture);
- *explicit awareness* (becoming aware of the mundane details that most people filter out of their routine observations);
- *a good memory* (because it is not always possible to record observations on the spot);
- *cultivated naïveté* (i.e. never being afraid to question the obvious or the taken-for-granted);
- *writing skills* (because ultimately most observational data will only be useful when placed in some sort of narrative context).

The process of observational research

'Observation' rarely involves a single act. Rather, it is a series of steps that builds toward the regularity and precision inherent in our working definition.

- The first step of the process is *site selection*. A site may be selected in order to respond to a theoretical question, or because it somehow represents an issue of current concern, or simply because it is convenient. However the site is selected, however, it is necessary for the researcher to
- *gain entrée* into the community. Some communities are open to outsiders, others less accommodating. If one needs to work in one of those less inviting settings, added preparations must be made. *Gatekeepers*, both formal (e.g. police, political officials) and informal (e.g. respected elders), must be approached and their approval and support gained.
- Once having gained access to the site, the individual researcher may begin observing immediately. Those working with teams may, however, need to take some time for training, just to make sure everyone is doing his or her assigned task in the proper manner. If one is working in a situation requiring the assistance of translators or others who live in the community, it may be necessary to spend some initial time orienting them to the goals and operations of the research project. It may also be necessary to take some time to become accustomed to the site. The more exotic the locale, the more likely will it be that the researcher suffers from *culture shock* – a sense of being overwhelmed by the new and unfamiliar. But even when working close to home in reasonably familiar surroundings, the

researcher may go through a phase of 'shock' just because he or she is inter-acting with that setting in the role of researcher in ways quite different from those that characterized earlier encounters.

- Once observation is underway, the researcher will probably find it necessary to make note of just about everything. An understanding of what is and is not central comes only after repeated observations (and probably also consulta-tions with members of the community). In any case, it is crucial that obser-vations be recorded in such a way as to facilitate retrieval of information. There is no universally accepted format for the recording of observational materials. Some researchers prefer highly structured checklists, grids, tables, and so forth; others prefer free-form narratives. Some like to enter data directly into computer software programs, others like to (or must, depending on local conditions) use manual means like notebooks, index cards, and so forth. The bottom line is that the method is best that helps the individual researcher retrieve and analyze whatever has been collected, and this stan-dard will necessarily vary from one researcher to another. Of course, group projects require a standardization of information recording, even if the method selected would not have been the first choice of some individual members of the team.
- As the research progresses, observations will gradually fall into discernible *patterns*, which suggest further questions to pursue, either through additional observations or other means of research. The anthropologist James Spradley (1980) has referred to the stages of observation as a 'funnel' because the process gradually narrows and directs researchers' attention more deeply into the elements of the setting that have emerged as essential, either on the theo-retical or the empirical level.
- Observations continue until a point of *theoretical saturation* is achieved. This means that the generic features of new findings consistently replicate earlier ones.

The question of validity

Quantitative researchers can demonstrate both the *validity* and the *reliability* of their data through statistical means. 'Reliability' is a measure of the degree to which any given observation is consistent with a general pattern and not the result of random chance. 'Validity' is a measure of the degree to which an observation actually demonstrates what it appears to demonstrate. Qualitative ethnographic researchers are not usually concerned with reliability, since they recognize the fact that much of what they do is, in the last analysis, not truly replicable. There is, in other words, no expectation that one researcher observing a community at one time will exactly duplicate the findings of a different researcher observing that same community at a different time. By contrast, a biologist observing cellular processes under a microscope should come up with standard results no matter who he or she is, when the observation was made, and so forth.

Nevertheless, there are some ways in which observation-based researchers can achieve something approaching criteria of scientific reliability. For example, observations that are conducted in a systematic fashion (i.e. using some sort of standardized technique for the recording and analysis of the data) and that are repeated regularly over a course of time can be considered credible if they yield roughly comparable results. The desire to approximate scientific reliability in observational research, however, represents a reliance on a view of social research as a species of science in which human behavior is 'lawful' and regular and can be objectively described and analyzed. Such a position would, of course, be considered irrelevant by postmodernists of various types, as discussed in an earlier chapter.

On the other hand, even postmodernists must be very concerned with validity; if there is no basis for trusting the observation, then the research is meaningless. The question of validity haunts qualitative research in general, but it poses particular problems for observation-based research. Observations are susceptible to bias from subjective interpretations. Unlike interview-based research, which can feature direct quotes from people in the community, observational findings are rarely 'confirmable'. Nevertheless, there are some ways that observational researchers can legitimize their work for their scientific peers. (Note that they may not have to do so for general or popular audiences, for whom the fact that the observer was 'there' and speaks with a voice of authority about what he or she has found out, is often good enough.) Some of the most commonly deployed means of achieving validity include the following:

- It is often advisable to work with *multiple observers* or teams (see also Flick, 2007b), particularly if they represent various viewpoints (e.g. gender, age, ethnic background); the members of such teams can cross-check each others' findings in order to discover and eliminate inaccuracies. Of course, an observer whose findings are not in agreement with those of his or her colleagues is not necessarily 'wrong'; he or she may, in fact, be the only one to have gotten it right. However, unless there is compelling reason to suspect that the loner/maverick is on to something important, the consensus of the group usually prevails.
- It may be possible to follow the methodology of *analytic induction* (see also Flick, 2007b), which in this case means that emergent propositions (findings that describe patterns in the observations) are tested in a search for negative cases. The goal is to achieve assertions that can be taken as universal (or 'grounded', in the language of some schools of theory).

- When writing up results, the observation-based researcher may be encouraged to use techniques of *verisimilitude* (or *vraisemblance*, a term that has come into English via French scholars). This is a style of writing that draws the reader into the world that has been studied so as to evoke a mood of recognition; it uses rich descriptive language (rather than abstract 'facts and figures'). Verisimilitude is also achieved when the description seems to be internally coherent, plausible, and recognizable by readers from their own experiences or from other things they have read or heard about. A work that achieves these goals is said to be *authentic* in the eyes of those who read it. In other words, more than other types of scientific 'data', ethnographic observations only become 'valid' when they have been rendered into some sort of coherent, consistent narrative.

The whole matter of standards for assuring the quality of research findings generated in non-quantified contexts has been studied extensively and summarized by Seale (1999). Guba and Lincoln (2005, pp. 205–9) provide both a brief review of the literature and a complex philosophical reflection on the question of validity in qualitative research. After considerable examination of the ways in which qualitative researchers collect data, including those who use observational and other ethnographic means to collect information, Miles and Huberman (1994, pp. 278–80) have come up with some practical 'pointers' (not 'rules', they carefully explain) to help us judge the quality of research conclusions. They divide their pointers into five basic categories:

- *Objectivity/confirmability* (or 'external reliability'): the degree to which conclusions flow from the information that has been collected, and not from any biases on the part of the researcher.
- *Reliability/dependability/auditability*: the degree to which the process of research has been consistent and reasonably stable over time and across various researchers and methods.
- *Internal validity/credibility/authenticity* (or 'truth value'): the degree to which the conclusions of a study make sense, if they are credible to the people studied as well as to readers of the report, and if the final product is an authentic record of whatever it was that was observed.
- *External validity/transferability/fittingness*: the degree to which the conclusions of a study have relevance to matters beyond the study itself (i.e. can the findings be generalized to other contexts?).
- *Utilization/application/action orientation* (the 'pragmatic validity' of a study): the degree to which programs or actions result from a study's findings and/or the degree to which ethical issues are forthrightly dealt with (for criteria in qualitative research more generally, see Flick, 2007b).

Observer bias

Ethnographers in general, and observation-based researchers in particular, are frequently criticized for the subjectivity that informs their work. Even the most apparently unobtrusive observation can have unintended 'observer effects' – the tendency of people to change their behavior because they know they are being observed. Most contemporary researchers would agree that it is inadvisable to seek to avoid all remnants of observer effects, since the only way to do so would be to return to the covert tactics of the 'complete observer' role, which has been widely criticized as potentially unethical. Nevertheless, there are some ways to minimize the bias that almost always enters into observational research:

- It might be said that the very *naturalness* of observation provides some inoculation against bias, since the observer (unlike the interviewer, for example) is usually not demanding that people do anything out of the ordinary. It is hoped that in time his or her presence will no longer even be a matter of note and that people will simply go about their business.
- Observational research is *emergent*, which in this context means that it has great potential for creativity. Observational researchers can, if they so choose, eschew predetermined categories; at any point in the process outlined above, the researcher can shift the question(s) he or she is pursuing. Observation has the potential to yield new insights as 'reality' comes into clearer focus as the result of experience in the field setting.
- Observational research combines well with other techniques for the collection of information. Laboratory or clinical experiments, for example, lack the natural setting and context of occurrence; they generate 'data' that are self-contained and from which all 'extraneous' variables have been rigorously excluded. But field-based ethnography is rarely constructed around a self-contained observational 'experiment'. Rather, observations are made of life as it is lived in the natural setting, and observational findings are constantly being cross-checked with information coming from interviews, archival searches, and so forth. This process of *triangulation*, which as we have seen is intrinsic to ethnography in general, is a good hedge against the biases that may result from 'pure' observation (see also Flick, 2007b).

Observations in public spaces

One of the most characteristic applications of observational research is that which is carried out in public spaces. Indeed, given the nature of this setting, observation is almost always the preferred technique, given the difficulty of arranging interviews in such a setting and the lack of archival back-up for a shifting, heterogeneous, ill-defined population. Traditional public space research, such as that of Erving Goffman, was carried out in the manner of the covert, 'complete outsider' role. Although that is no longer necessarily so, public spaces remain a distinctive 'field' for observational research.

Some public spaces are fairly clearly delineated (e.g. airport waiting rooms, shopping malls), others less so (e.g. busy downtown streets), but all provide the context for studies involving moral order, interpersonal relations, and norms for dealing with different categories of individuals, including total strangers. A case can be made that in urban society, public spaces are an ideal setting for research in that they represent a microcosm of the dense, heterogeneous – even dangerous – society at large. People in urban societies do seem to spend a large part of their lives in public, so much so that formerly private functions (e.g. talking on a phone) are now commonly carried out in public. It is mainly in smaller-scale traditional societies where we still find the core activities carried on behind closed doors, as it were – private spaces to which we do not have immediate observational access. As such, observational studies in public spaces allow researchers to gather data on large groups of people and thereby to identify patterns of group behavior.

It may be said that the anonymity and alienation of life in a modern urban environment lead people to create enclaves of private space within the larger public context; even people crammed together in an elevator will typically stand in rigid postures, to convey the message that they are not interested in touching anyone else. Nevertheless, when people leave those small protected spaces and go out into the larger public space beyond, they must go forth with sufficient knowledge about the potential range of social types they might have to deal with; in other words, they have to know how to deal with the actions of strangers. In traditional societies, it was generally assumed that strangers could never be trusted because one never knew how to 'read' them. But in urban society, where almost everyone is a stranger, it would be dysfunctional to treat everyone as a massive, collective unknown. So we learn to put people into categories or types, and we respond to those types even if we do not personally know the individual representatives of those types. Of course, doing so inevitably leads to stereotyping, with occasionally unfortunate consequences. But that is the trade-off most people make in order to be able to negotiate a potentially threatening environment.

Perhaps the most famous – even notorious – example of public space observational research is that of Humphreys (1975), who adopted a covert observer-as-participant role in a public bathroom. His intention was to observe men engaging in impersonal homosexual encounters. Using a very structured methodology of data recording, he concluded that men in this setting adopt one of several possible roles, which he described as waiter, voyeur, masturbator, insertor, and insertee. He also meticulously recorded the characteristics of participants and their relations with their temporary partners, as well as with potentially dangerous outsiders. The provocative nature of Humphreys's study raised eyebrows at the time of its publication, and it continues to be an object-lesson in the ethics of observational research, a topic to which we will now return, using this study as a case example.

Ethics and observational research

General questions of research ethics as they apply to ethnography are treated in a later chapter, but a few special points need to be dealt with in this focused discussion of observation.

On the one hand, the relatively unobtrusive nature of observational research lessens the opportunities for unfavorable interpersonal encounters between researcher and 'subjects'. But it is that very quality of unobtrusiveness that opens it to abuse in the form of the invasion of privacy. A researcher can be guilty of the latter either by entering into places that can be construed as private even though they have a public character (e.g. a public bathroom) or by intruding into the zone of privacy carved out by people within the larger public space (e.g. eavesdropping on what is clearly a private conversation although it takes place right next to you at a busy lunch counter). It may also occur through a researcher misrepresenting him or herself as a member of the group he or she wants to observe. Doing so is not necessarily a serious problem (although it is still an ethical violation) if the group is not defensive about its own identity; for example, a researcher posing as a passenger by surrounding him or herself with luggage in order to observe an airport waiting room is not doing violence to anyone's integrity. However, if the group has a stigmatized identity, or if it is engaged in criminal activities or activities thought of by others as somehow deviant, then pretending to be an insider can represent a very significant violation of the privacy of others.

Some researchers question the general application of this rule of non-violation of privacy, asking whether conforming to the rule automatically eliminates certain sensitive – but obviously socially important – subjects (e.g. sex) from the research agenda. The usual answer is that studying sensitive subjects is not taboo – but doing so without the express permission of the participants is ethically wrong. In any case, it is now generally agreed that:

- It is unethical for a researcher to deliberately misrepresent his or her identity for the purpose of entering a private domain to which he or she is not otherwise eligible.
- It is unethical for a researcher to deliberately misrepresent the character of the research in which he or she is engaged. (See Erikson, 1967, for an exposition of these principles.)

These reflections bring us back to Humphreys's research. At the time of its publication, his book would have been controversial enough given its subject matter, which was not common in the social research of that period, and which was seen as downright titillating by the general public. But criticism was not at first directed at Humphreys's activities as an observer. Rather, they concerned the way he continued his research beyond the bathroom. Among the data he so carefully collected were the license plates of the men he observed in the bathroom. After his stint of observation, he tracked down as many of them as he could using their plate numbers, and arranged to conduct interviews with them. He had changed his looks and identified himself as being part of a public health survey. He did not reveal that he had covertly encountered them before. Although he was only collecting demographic data – innocuous in and of themselves – and not prying into the details of their sex lives, the fact that he was able to connect men involved in an illicit activity with their larger demographic context, and that he was able to do so without their knowledge, let alone their permission, was seen as a very worrisome matter.

Scrutiny of this aspect of his research led many to revisit the original observational study itself. When in the bathroom, Humphreys tried out a few of the roles for himself, including that of straight person/bystander and 'waiter'. Neither of these poses got him the access he needed. So he decided to take on the role of 'watchqueen', essentially a look-out. In that guise he came to be trusted by the others, who were unaware that his agenda entailed making careful observations of their behavior and only incidentally warning them of approaching danger. As 'watchqueen', Humphreys could take on a recognized and valued membership role that nonetheless stopped short of his participation in the sexual activity going on around him. Humphreys's critics pointed out that he was ethically wrong to have misrepresented himself deliberately as a member in order to gain access. Moreover, it was said that he put his needs as a researcher ahead of the rights of the people he was studying. He did not pay sufficient attention to the consequences should his research be made public in ways he could not control. He had not even considered the possibility that the police, should they find out what he was doing, might subpoena his notes in order to bring criminal charges against the men in his study.

The Humphreys case is perhaps an extreme one. Most observational researchers do not venture into such a moral danger zone, and when they do they are presumably armed with the ethical precautions now mandated by law (see Chapter 8 for an elaboration of these measures). But it is important to remember that even when a situation is not as obviously controversial as a public bathroom, ethics can arise when observation is covert and the identity of the researcher is misrepresented.

In sum, 'researchers are reminded that they must take into account subjects' rights to freedom from manipulation when weighing the potential benefits of the research role against the harms that could accrue' (Adler and Adler, 1994, p. 389).

======= **Key points**

- Observation is the act of noting a phenomenon, often with instruments, and recording it for scientific purposes.
- Ethnographers using observational techniques in their research may adopt roles ranging from that of the complete observer to the complete participant, although most opt for participant or membership roles that fall between these extremes.
- Observational research is not a single act, but rather a developmental process involving

  ✓ site selection
  ✓ the gaining of entrée into the community
  ✓ the training of co-workers and/or local participants, as necessary
  ✓ note-taking:

    ➢ structured
    ➢ narrative

  ✓ discernment of patterns
  ✓ achievement of theoretical saturation, a state in which generic features of new findings consistently replicate earlier ones.

- The *reliability* of observational research is a matter of systematic recording and analysis of data and the repetition of observations regularly over a course of time.
- The *validity* of observational research is a means of determining the authenticity of the findings. It can be stated in terms of

  ✓ multiple observers
  ✓ analytic induction
  ✓ verisimilitude.

- Observer bias may be mitigated because observational research is

  ✓ natural
  ✓ emergent
  ✓ combined with other techniques.

- Observations carried out in public spaces are subject to stringent ethical oversight because of the potential for abuse of subjects' right to privacy.

  ✓ It is unethical for a researcher to deliberately misrepresent his or her identity for the purpose of entering a private domain to which he or she is not otherwise eligible.
  ✓ It is unethical for a researcher to deliberately misrepresent the character of the research in which he or she is engaged.

65

Further reading

These texts elasorate on the issues mentioned in this chapter:

Bernard, H.R. (1988) *Research Methods in Cultural Anthropology*. Newbury Park, CA: Sage.

Flick, U. (2007b) *Managing Quality in Qualitative Research* (Book 8 of *The SAGE Qualitative Research Kit*). London: Sage.

Schensul, S.L., Schensul, J.J. and LeCompte, M.D. (1999) *Essential Ethnographic Methods: Observations, Interviews, and Questionnaires* (Vol. II of J.J. Schensul, S.L. Schensul and M.D. LeCompte, (eds), *Ethnographer's Toolkit*). Walnut Creek, CA: AltaMira.

Spradley, J.P. (1980) *Participant Observation*. New York: Holt, Rinehart & Winston.

6
Analyzing ethnographic data

Chapter objectives
After reading this chapter you should

- be familiar with the ways in which the data collected through ethnographic research can be systematically searched for patterns; and
- know in which ways those patterns can be explained and used as the basis for further research.

Having used the various data collection techniques discussed in the previous chapter either singly or (preferably) in combination, the researcher is faced with the question of what to do with that considerable amount of information. Some of it will be numerical (e.g. the result of formal ethnographic surveys), but much of it is likely to be in narrative form (i.e. the result of in-depth interviews, or the notes resulting from structured observations). Regardless of what conventional wisdom tells us, *the facts do not speak for themselves*. Even numerical data need to be interpreted. The collected data need to be *analyzed* so that some sort of sense will emerge from all that information. We cannot therefore speak of how to collect data in ethnographic research without also considering how to analyze those data.

There are two main forms of data analysis:

- *Descriptive analysis* is the process of taking the stream of data and breaking it down into its component parts; in other words, what patterns, regularities, or themes emerge from the data?

- *Theoretical analysis* is the process of figuring out how those component parts fit together; in other words, how can we explain the existence of patterns in the data, or how do we account for the perceived regularities?

Patterns

How do you recognize a pattern? Basically speaking, a true pattern is one that is shared by members of the group (their *actual* behavior) and/or one that is believed to be desirable, legitimate, or proper by the group (their *ideal* behavior). We can systematize the recognition of patterns by going through the following steps:

- Consider each *statement* made by someone in the community you are study-ing. Was it: (a) made to others in everyday conversation, or (b) elicited by you in an interview?
- For each of those two conditions, consider whether it was: (a) volunteered by the person, or (b) directed in some way by you.
- Consider each *activity* that you have observed. Did it: (a) occur when you were alone with a single individual, or (b) occur when you were in the pres-ence of a group?
- For each of those two conditions, consider whether: (a) the person or group acted spontaneously, or (b) acted because of some prompt on your part.

In general, public statements and actions are more likely to reflect the ideal behavior of the group than are those expressed in private. Statements and activ-ities that occur spontaneously or are volunteered by the people in the community are more likely to be elements in a shared pattern than are those somehow prompted by the researcher.

When conducting ethnographic research in the field, we always have to remember that we are not in control of all the elements in the research process: we are capturing life as it is being lived, and hence we must be aware that things that might appear meaningful to us as outsiders might or might not be equally meaningful to the people who live in the community being studied – and vice versa. Social scientists (anthropologists in particular) refer to the two perspec-tives on meaning as the *emic* and the *etic*. These terms come from the field of lin-guistics, where phon*emic* analysis refers to the delineation of sounds that convey meaning to native speakers of a language while phon*etic* analysis converts all sounds into a kind of international code system that allows for the comparative understanding of meanings. So in the simplest sense, an 'emic' perspective on social and cultural data is that which looks for the patterns, themes, and regular-ities as they are perceived by the people who live in the community; an 'etic' per-spective is one that is applied by the researcher (who will have at least read about, if not actually conducted first-hand fieldwork in many other communities) interested in seeing how what goes on locally compares to things happening elsewhere.

Field-based researchers try to engage in a *constant validity check*, which basically involves switching back and forth between emic and etic perspectives. Like so many other processes that we have discussed, constant validity checking seems like a reasonably straightforward, intuitive activity; the trick, as usual, is to learn to do it in a systematic fashion. There are some important elements in the process:

- Look for both consistencies and inconsistencies in what knowledgeable informants tell you; probe for why people living in the same community might disagree about matters that seem to be significant to them.
- Check what people in the community say about behaviors or events against other evidence, if available (e.g. newspaper accounts, reports by others who have conducted fieldwork in the same community, or one very similar to it). But remember that even if what people say is factually 'wrong', their views are not irrelevant; try to find out why they persist in holding 'erroneous' views.
- Be open to 'negative evidence'. If a case arises that doesn't fit your own emerging etic view, try to find out why this discrepancy exists. Is it the result of simple variation within the culture of the community? Does it reflect your own lack of knowledge about the community? Is it a true anomaly that would stick out even in an emic perspective (see Flick, 2007b)?
- Play with alternative explanations for patterns that seem to be emerging. Do not wed yourself to a single analytical framework before all the data are in hand.

The process of data analysis

There is no single formula accepted by all ethnographic researchers that can serve as a strategy for the analysis of data collected in the field (see Gibbs, 2007). Indeed, some scholars have made the point that the analysis of data (quantified data excepted) is necessarily 'custom-built' to suit the particular needs of specific projects. Ethnographic data analysis may thus seem to be more of an art than a science and certainly ethnographers have been accused of being 'soft' scientists (i.e. intuitive and impressionistic, rather than rigorous in their analysis). But there is more regularity in their approaches than might initially be apparent, and several important points are found in most formulations of the process. They may be taken as an outline for an acceptable framework for analysis. Keep in mind, however, that the 'steps' in this framework need not happen in a strictly sequential order. They may happen simultaneously, or some of them may have to be repeated in the course of the research.

- *Data management.* As noted in the previous chapter, it is essential to keep clearly organized field notes. More and more contemporary ethnographers find it convenient to keep their notes in the form of computer files. But low-tech field workers are still to be found (sometimes because the circumstances of their field settings are not congenial to the use of computers, other times simply out of habit and preference) using paper file folders or index cards. I personally like to use loose-leaf notebooks with category dividers, which keep notes all in one place but allow for them to be moved as needed. No one method is better than any other – it all depends on how you like to work. The most important thing is that you be able to find and retrieve data once you have filed it, regardless of what your filing format might be (see Gibbs, 2007, for a further discussion of these matters).
- *Overview reading.* It is usually a good idea to read through your notes before proceeding with more formal analysis. There may be details you have for-gotten since you first collected the data, and an overview reading will refresh your memory. It will also stimulate you to begin reflecting on what you think you now know, and to begin asking questions about what you still want to understand.
- *Clarification of categories.* Begin with a *description* of what you have seen in your notes. Then move to a *classification* of the notes, a process of taking apart the narrative description and identifying categories or themes. Sometimes you can identify themes on the basis of your review of the scholarly litera-ture on the topic(s) you are investigating. Keep in mind that the 'literature' pertinent to your study includes theoretical analyses and methodological explorations in addition to ethnographies in similar communities. In other cases, you will have no preconceived themes, but allow them to emerge from your reading of the data. In either case, begin with no more than six themes. If you have too many themes, every incident forms its own category and you have gained nothing; if you have too few themes, you risk conflating statements or behaviors that might prove to be distinct. You can always reconfigure your thematic categories as you go along, but in a preliminary pass-through you need something to get you started.

In the Trinidad study, I was able to draw upon a fairly extensive body of exist-ing literature on the international Indian indenture. From that literature I identi-fied several key themes that were helpful in organizing my own data: the loss of caste; changes in family structure; the role of traditional religions; economic opportunities in the post-indenture period; political relations between Indians and others in the post-colonial society; secondary migration (i.e. second- or third-generation Indians leaving the place of indenture for England, Canada, or the United States). I organized my notebook using these themes as major categories. Upon reading my notes in preparation for analysis of the final results, I realized what I had already begun to suspect: that the first category was more or less a non-issue among the Trinidad Indians, and that except for Brahmins (the religious specialists) not even the most elderly people could accurately remember their traditional caste affiliations and no one seemed very concerned that this supposed pillar of Indian culture had disappeared over the generations of the indenture. So other than affirming that, yes, there had been a 'loss of caste' in the community I had studied, just as there had been in other communities studied in other parts of the overseas Indian world, I had little in my notes to sustain this as a usable category. On the other hand, alcoholism had clearly emerged as an overriding issue. My many notes on interviews and observations of AA meetings that were scattered through the existing categories were taken out and put in their own separate category. It thus became possible to compare and contrast alcoholism against such predisposing factors as religion, family, and economic and political relationships. The generation of these categories was initially 'etic' because they derived from the comparative literature on the indenture. But the later modifications of the categories reflected an 'emic' emphasis, responding as they did to what my informants had demonstrated to me as being important to them.

In the deinstitutionalization study, I opted against using ready-made categories based on the existing literature since so much of the literature derived from clinically based research and/or research conducted among the professional caretakers of people with mental disabilities. My own ethnographic study of the people themselves would undoubtedly yield a somewhat different perspective. So during the course of my research I kept my notes in the form of a running narrative somewhat like a diary (minus the personal reflections, which I reserved to a separate private journal). I also kept separately transcriptions of each extended interview. Such a format would obviously be unusable when the time came to write up my findings, and so it was necessary to do a very thorough overview reading and then define the categories that jumped out, namely: sexuality; finding and keeping a job; relations with family; relations with friends; relations with professionals; world-views (i.e. how they saw themselves and interpreted their place in the 'wider scheme of things'). The generation of these categories was almost entirely 'emic' since it was guided for the most part by what the people had told me.

- *Presentation of data.* With the data arranged into useful categories, it is possible to summarize them in text, tabular, or figure form (or some combination of those formats). There are several commonly used presentation forms.

  ✓ *The* 'comparison table' *or matrix.* This can be as simple as a 2 × 2 table that compares two segments of a population in terms of one of the categories, e.g.

71

| Hindu Indians | Member of AA | Not member of AA |
| Muslim Indians | Member of AA | Not member of AA |

✓ The actual cells would be filled with descriptive text as well as numbers in this case. Such a table made it clear (in a way that was much less obvious in the raw notes) that on a numerical level there were more Muslims in AA than would be expected from the simple demographics. In the general population, Hindus accounted for approximately 80 per cent of the Indian population, while Muslims made up approximately 15 per cent, the remainder being Christian converts. But Muslims accounted for 35 per cent of the Indian AA membership, while Hindus were at 60 per cent, with the remainder Christian. The accompanying text helped explain why Muslims were relatively more attracted to AA. In interviews, many of them commented on the fact that as a sub-community within the larger Indian population they had always considered themselves 'more progressive' than the Hindus, and they saw joining AA as a 'modern' response to their problem. Those comments did not stand out until placed in this comparison table in which the numbers indicated an unexpected pattern, which the narrative text helped explicate.

✓ *The hierarchical tree.* This diagram shows different levels of abstraction. The top of the tree represents the most abstract information and the bottom the least abstract. For example, in explaining the indenture, the highest level of abstraction reflected two large-scale perspectives: the political-economic (conditions relative to the powerlessness of colonized people and to the specific deprivations resulting from decades of servitude) and the psychological (conditions relative to the loss of traditional cultural identity-markers). A middle level reflected the kinds of stress that are found in a transplanted, economically exploited, politically disenfranchised population (e.g. a perceived disparity between the group's aspirations and the social resources available to realize those aspirations). At the bottom were the specific data relative to the experiences of the Indians in Trinidad in whose community I was a participant observer.

✓ *Hypotheses or propositions.* These statements of relationship need not be formally tested (as in quantitative research), but arranging the thematic elements in the data in such a format can certainly clarify the ways the perceived variables fit together. For example, I could state the proposition that adult men with mental retardation who have active family ties are more apt to complete their community habilitation programs than are those with weak ties. Since I was obviously in no position to identify, let alone examine, anything near to a statistically representative sample of adult men with mental retardation, I could not hope to test this hypothesis in a meaningful way. But the simple statement of relationship was a way of organizing my data and understanding the life experiences of the men I was able to work with.

✓ *Metaphors*. Metaphors are literary devices, shorthand ways of expressing relationships. (I like to think of them as poetic versions of hypotheses.) For example, one of my AA informants used the phrase 'inside is life, outside is death'. He was speaking specifically about AA because he believed that if he left the group he would certainly go back to drinking and that doing so would kill him. But I also understood him to be reflecting a more general attitude among Indians, who found security in their own community and saw the outside world as a political, economic, and cultural threat. For Indians, 'inside' included family, religion, and jobs in the sugar industry as well as AA, while 'outside' included the political system of modern Trinidad, jobs in the oil industry, and hospital-based forms of rehabilitation. My informant's metaphorical division of the world proved to be a very useful way to sort out my own data, and I ultimately used the phrase 'outside is death' as the title of the book that came from that research project. In a somewhat more blunt use of metaphors, one of the men in the community retardation program told me in some exasperation, 'My life is a toilet.' He meant that he counted as a waste everything he had ever done. One could take the remark at face value as nothing more than a cry of frustration or desperation. But it was also possible to use it as a key to unlock a whole set of observational and interview data: *Why* was life a waste? It became clearer to me in interrogating that metaphor that this man – and many of his compatriots – considered life a waste because they were not truly adult (not 'real people', as they often said). They were not trusted to do the things adults do (including most definitely to express their sexuality) and so everything they did was by definition childish and worthless.

So we can summarize the analysis process as follows beginning with the *descriptive analysis* phase:

- Organize notes, using thematic categories drawn from the literature if possible.
- Read through the notes and modify categories as necessary.
- Sort data into the modified categories.
- Count the number of entries in each category for purposes of descriptive statistical analysis (if the sample is large enough to permit it).
- Look for patterns in textual materials, using a variety of presentation formats as aids.

Next, we can consider the *theoretical analysis*:

- Consider the patterns in light of existing literature.
- Demonstrate how your findings relate to the interpretations of others. (Your findings may confirm what is already known and add new illustrative examples to an established perspective. Or they may run counter to the expectations and thus stimulate further research. Either option is a legitimate and praiseworthy outcome; see also Gibbs, 2007, for analyzing qualitative data).

A note on the use of computers in ethnographic data analysis

In relatively small-scale research projects, the amount of data may be manageable manually, i.e. it might be possible simply to 'eyeball' patterns. But projects that generate a very large amount of data can certainly benefit from one of the several computer software programs now available that are designed to aid the process of analysis (see Gibbs, 2007).

The most basic computer function for researchers is *word processing*. Programs such as Word or Word Perfect do not merely serve when it comes to writing up final reports. They also allow users to create text-based files, and to find, move, reproduce, and retrieve sections of those texts. Word processing is also important when it comes to transcribing interviews, keeping track of field notes, and coding text for purposes of indexing and retrieval.

Word processing is familiar to most of us nowadays, but there are other kinds of software that might be of assistance to the ethnographic researcher. *Text retrievers* (e.g. Orbis, ZyINDEX) specialize in locating each occurrence of a specified word or phrase; they can also locate combinations of these items in multiple files. *Textbase managers* (e.g. Tabletop) refine the text retrieval function and have an enhanced capacity for the organization of textual data. *Code-and-retrieve programs* (QUALPRO, Ethnograph) assist researchers in dividing text into manageable sections, which can then be sorted. *Code-based theory builders* (e.g. ATLAS/ti, NUD.IST) go beyond code-and-retrieve functions and permit the development of theoretical connections between and among coded concepts, resulting in relatively high-order classifications and connections. *Conceptual network builders* (e.g. SemNet) provide the capacity to design graphic networks in which variables are displayed as 'nodes' that are linked to one another using arrows or lines denoting relationships. (Weitzman and Miles, 1995, describe these computer-based research functions, although given the rapidity with which technology develops, the reader is well advised to consult up-to-date websites containing the most recent information about specific programs; see also Gibbs, 2007, for the use of software for qualitative analysis.)

Pros of computerized data analysis:

- The computer program itself is a form of organized data storage, making it that much easier to retrieve material.
- Sorting and searching for text is done automatically and in far less time than would be consumed doing so manually.
- The program requires a careful (virtually line-by-line) examination of the data. In ordinary reading, it is possible to skim and thus lose potentially important pieces of information.

Cons of computerized data analysis:

- There might be a steep (and time-inefficient) learning curve for new software programs. And let's face it, some people are still just not comfortable around computers.
- Although they function best as adjuncts to traditional, manual means of analysis, computer programs tempt the researcher to let them do *all* the work.
- There are many data analysis programs now available to the ethnographic researcher, but they do not all do the same thing. It is possible to spend a lot of money acquiring a program and then spend a lot of time learning how to operate it, only to discover that it doesn't really do what you need it to do. Do your homework about the programs before you commit yourself to one or another.

Key points

- The facts do not speak for themselves. Analysis of data is thus an integral part of the process of data collection.
- There are two main forms of data analysis:
  - ✓ descriptive (the search for patterns)
  - ✓ theoretical (the search for meaning in the patterns).

- Patterns may be discerned through an
  - ✓ emic perspective (how do the people under study understand things?)
  - ✓ etic perspective (how can the researcher link data from the community under study to similar cases conducted elsewhere?).

- Ethnographers engage in a constant validity check, which involves letting emic and etic perspectives comment on each other.
- Although there is no one consensus format for the analysis of ethnographic data, a workable framework might consist of

- ✓ data management
- ✓ overview reading
- ✓ clarification of categories:

    - ➢ description
    - ➢ classification

- ✓ presentation of data:

    - ➢ matrix (comparison table)
    - ➢ hierarchical tree
    - ➢ hypotheses (propositions)
    - ➢ metaphors.

- Computer software is now widely available to assist the ethnographic researcher in the analysis of data.

Further reading

The following books give you more information about analyzing observational data, and in particular about using computers and software for this purpose:

Babbie, E. (1986) *Observing Ourselves: Essays in Social Research.* Prospect Heights, IL: Waveland.

Gibbs, G.R. (2007) *Analyzing Qualitative Data* (Book 6 of *The SAGE Qualitative Research Kit*). London: Sage.

LeCompte, M.D. and Schensul, J.J. (1999) *Designing and Conducting Ethnographic Research.* (Vol. I of J.J. Schensul, S.L. Schensul and M.D. LeCompte, (eds), *Ethnographer's Toolkit*). Walnut Creek, CA: AltaMira.

Weitzman, E.A. and Miles, M.B. (1995) *Computer Programs for Qualitative Data Analysis.* Thousand Oaks, CA: Sage.

7
Strategies for representing ethnographic data

Chapter objectives
After reading this chapter you should

- know some of the ways in which ethnographers can convey their findings to the public;
- see that standard scientific monographs are now often supplemented by forms of 'alternative ethnography'; and
- know about representations of ethnographic data in forms other than writing.

Collecting data in ethnographic research yields a pile of 'facts' which, as we have seen, do not speak for themselves. They must be analyzed so that their sense is clarified. For that reason we said that data analysis is an integral part of the data collection process.

We can take this logic one step further. There seems to be little point in collecting data and then analyzing it so that clear patterns emerge for the researcher to account for unless those conclusions are conveyed to some audience. There may be a kind of pleasure to be had in doing research strictly for one's own private edification, but for the most part researchers – most definitely including ethnographers – engage in research so that they can be part of an ongoing dialogue with other scholars, and often with general audiences beyond academe.

It is often assumed that the only logical way to represent ethnographic data to an interested audience is in the form of the traditional work of scholarly writing – the book or monograph, the article for the scientific journal, the paper to be read at a meeting of a professional society. And so we will consider in this chapter some of the standards that apply to the production of such a scholarly work of ethnography. But we will also consider options that are increasingly available to the ethnographic researcher – alternative ways of representing their data so as to communicate with an ever-widening potential audience.

Representing ethnographic data in traditional scholarly form

Scientific writing of whatever length typically includes several key elements usually set out in a conventional order. (Berg, 2004, pp. 299–317, provides a very clear exposition of the principles of writing a scholarly ethnographic paper; see also Creswell, 1994, pp. 193–208.)

- A *title* is a direct description of what the report is about; it should not be overly 'cute' or 'clever', although an ethnographic report may use in its title a colorful quote from someone in the study community.
- An *abstract* is a brief (100–200 words) overview of the research that features the most important findings and mentions the methods by which data were collected and analyzed and closes with a statement of the implications of the major findings. There is little or no explanation or illustrative detail in the abstract (which in a book-length work may be replaced by a *preface* of relatively greater length and involving a little more detail).
- An *introduction* orients the reader/listener to the study; it includes a statement explaining (and perhaps justifying) the main research questions and an overview of the key issues that will be discussed.
- A *literature review* critically examines the published materials relevant to the research (substantively, methodologically, and theoretically); special emphasis is given to the studies that have the most direct bearing on the report at hand. The literature review is usually also the place where the author's own theoretical framework is explained and justified.
- A *methodological review* describes the author's procedures for data collection and analysis. The research setting may also be described in some detail; this element in the review is of particular importance in ethnographic research, since characteristics of the setting will be directly relevant to what is said to go on there.
- A report of *findings or results* links the study at hand in some way to the research questions posed in the introduction and to the issues that emerged from the literature review.
- A *concluding discussion* summarizes the main findings, fits the research into the literature, and suggests directions for future research.
- *References, notes, appendices* are explanatory materials supplemental to the main body of the text. Depending on the preference of journal editors or book

publishers, notes may be part of the text, placed at the foot of a page, or grouped at the end of a chapter (or of an entire book). In any case, notes must never convey substantive material that could just as well be in the text; references are to all cited material (although there may be a separate section of 'works not cited but consulted by the researcher' with the editor's approval) and must follow the standard form of the journal or publishing firm. Appended materials might include charts or tables, copies of original documents, photos, or any other matter that supports the main elements of the text.

Other ways of representing ethnographic data in writing

Although ethnography is a science, it is different in many ways from the 'hard' sciences (which are based on an experimental model of research and strive for strict objectivity through quantified data analysis). Ethnographers after all are often participant observers in the lives of the people they study; they bring a degree of subjectivity to the subject that would be considered inappropriate in a science like chemistry or physics. The traditional scientific style of writing has always been something of a straitjacket for the ethnographer who is, after all, trying to represent the lived experiences of real people. Gradually finding release from the confines of strict scientific writing, ethnographers have in recent years been experimenting with various forms of 'alternative' ethnographic writing, employing to one degree or another the forms of literature and the other arts in order to achieve a more expressive representation of the lived experiences of the people they study. There are increasing numbers of ethnographic reports that take the form of personal ('reflexive') narratives (i.e. the private diary achieving public form), short stories, novels, poems, or plays. These literary-influenced works fall into several main categories (sometimes referred to as 'tales'). (Van Maanen, 1988, is the standard reference for the discussion of ethnographic 'tales'. See also Sparkes, 2002, for an interesting alternative take on this same material.)

- *Realist tales* are characterized by extensive, closely edited quotations from the people who have been observed or interviewed with the intention of helping the reader 'hear' the actual voices of the people whose lives are being represented. Realist tales demonstrate a marked absence of the author, who disappears behind the words, actions, and (presumed) thoughts of the people he or she has studied. The realist tale has long and deep roots in ethnographic representation, with the work of Malinowski (1922) in the Trobriand Islands the classic example. In realist tales, the fieldworker is required to be a 'sober, civil, legal, dry, serious, dedicated transcriber of the world studied' (van Maanen, 1988, p. 55).

- *Confessional tales* are those in which the researcher steps forward and becomes a fully realized character in his or her narrative. The act of conducting participant observation research is described along with the description of the community under study. Confessional tales rarely stand alone; rather, confessional passages are typically inserted into conventional realist narratives. Manuals elaborating on how to conduct ethnographic research are often rich in confessional tales, as authors frequently use their own fieldwork experiences as cautionary material (see, e.g., Agar, 1980).

- *Autoethnography*, or the 'narrative of self', is a hybrid literary form in which the researcher uses his or her own personal experience as the basis of analysis. Autoethnographies are characterized by dramatic recall, strong metaphors, vivid characters, unusual phrasings, and the holding back of interpretation so as to invite the reader to relive the emotions experienced by the author. Ellis (1995), for example, has written an extended narrative dealing with the death of a significant other in her life, and the ways in which she dealt with being his caregiver. The details are highly particular to the case at hand, but Ellis's narrative style carefully links these specific concerns to general themes of life, death, and loss in our society. (See Ellis and Bochner, 1996, pp. 49–200, for a discussion and further case examples of autoethnographic representations.)

- *Poetic representations* are forms of expression typical of the community under study that are employed to give the reader a sense of how those people 'see' the world around them. For example, Richardson (1992) constructed a five-page poem about the life of an unmarried, Southern, rural, Christian woman from a poor family. The poem was based on a thirty-six-page interview transcript and was composed with careful attention to the voice, tone, rhythms, and diction of a person of this woman's time, place, and social station. Moreover, the poem used only the lady's own words.

- *Ethnodrama* is the transformation of data into theater scripts or performance pieces, which may include dance, mime, or other forms of expressive performance. For example, Mienczakowski (1996) sought to enhance community understanding of mental health and addiction issues. To that end, he created two plays based on his ethnographic research. The plays were performed at sites calculated to allow them to reach their optimal target audiences. Cast members included people drawn from the health professions as well as students of theater.

- *Fiction* is any literary form in which the setting and the people who were studied in that setting are represented fictionally (e.g. use of composite characters, setting characters in hypothetical events, attributing revelatory interior monologues to people when the researcher could not possibly have heard the original discourse). Fiction is sometimes employed for ethical reasons (the better to disguise the identities of people who might be compromised if they were too readily identified by conventionally 'objective' writing), sometimes to make a better link between the experiences of the study community and more universal concerns. My own account of research among mentally retarded adults (Angrosino, 1998) is an example of the translation of ethnographic data into the form of short stories. (See Banks and Banks, 1998, for a detailed critical discussion of the theory and method of fictional representation; this volume also contains several examples of ethnographic reporting translated into fictional terms.) In light of several recent controversies that have made front-page news, it should be stressed that when we speak of fictional representations of ethnographic data, it does *not* mean that we are talking about making things up and disguising them as facts. Fictional representation merely refers to the use of the techniques of literary fiction, rather than the conventions of academic prose, to tell a story; by general consensus, works of ethnographic fiction are clearly labeled as such.

It should be clear that these various forms of alternative ethnographic writing have the potential to reach audiences beyond the scholarly community. (See Richardson, 1990, perhaps the most frequently cited discussion of this issue.) As such, they may be less rigorous than we have grown used to in terms of their literature reviews or their explications of methodology and theory. But on the other hand, they can reach and move people and teach them about the experiences of others in ways that would never be possible with the standard scientific monograph, which is, after all, read only by other initiated scientists.

Beyond the written word

The *filmed documentary* has long been seen as a valid way to represent ethnographic data, although film production requires a set of highly specialized skills that are not often mastered by social science researchers. That situation may change now that video recording equipment has become such a familiar part of our technological landscape. Ethnographers might also think of expressive, fictional films in addition to objective documentaries, much as 'alternative' ethnographic writers have learned to use poetic or other fictional literary means to go beyond the, sometimes sterile, images typical of scientific writing. (See Heider, 1976, a relatively early, but still highly influential introduction to the use of film in ethnographic research.)

By the same token, the increasing popularity of digital photographic equipment has made it possible not only to produce high-quality images but also to disseminate them far more widely than was ever imagined. The *posting of both text and images on the Internet* is now a very real possibility for ethnographers. As was once the case with film, such web-based representations are still generally thought of as adjuncts to scholarly publication, although that situation may also change as more and more people have access to the web and seem to prefer it to other means of communication (see Bird, 2003). The *museum or other visual display/exhibit* is another way to represent ethnographic data in a vivid and widely appealing format (see Nanda, 2002).

It is beyond the scope of this book to describe in detail the how-to of these non-written forms of ethnographic representation, but the reader is urged to consider their possibilities for their own research. It is still a good idea to master first the skills of solid, traditional scientific writing. But then allow yourself to think about – and carry out – something more creative.

Key points

- Ethnographic data that are collected and analyzed must logically be represented in ways that convey information to some designated audience.
- The standard form of representation is the piece of scholarly writing (book/monograph, journal article, paper read at professional meeting). It generally consists of:

  ✓ title
  ✓ abstract
  ✓ introduction
  ✓ literature review
  ✓ methodological review
  ✓ report of findings or results
  ✓ concluding discussion
  ✓ references, notes, appendices.

- Ethnographic data can also be represented in alternative forms of writing, including

  ✓ realist tales
  ✓ confessional tales
  ✓ autoethnography
  ✓ poetic representations
  ✓ ethnodrama
  ✓ fiction.

- Non-written forms of representation include

  ✓ documentary films
  ✓ fictional films
  ✓ web-based text and images
  ✓ museum or other visual displays.

Further reading

These books go into more details of writing about ethnographic research and its findings:

Banks, A and Banks, S.P. (eds) (1998) *Fiction and Social Research: By Ice or Fire*. Walnut Creek, CA: AltaMira.

Ellis, C. and Bochner, A.P. (eds) (1996) *Composing Ethnography: Alternative Forms of Qualitative Writing*. Walnut Creek, CA: AltaMira.

Richardson, L. (1990) *Writing Strategies: Reaching Diverse Audiences*. Newbury Park, CA: Sage.

8
Ethical considerations

Chapter objectives
After reading this chapter you should know more about

- the ethics of conducting ethnographic fieldwork;
- standards of ethical research that are currently applied to all social scientists; and
- the special issues involved with participant observation.

Ethnographic research involving participant observation necessarily involves the direct interaction of researchers and those they study. Such close interaction can produce situations in which members of the study population are inadvertently harmed in some way. As a result, contemporary researchers are very concerned with the proper ethical conduct of research. One cannot legitimately discuss data collection in the ethnographic setting without also discussing the ethical dimension of that research.

Levels of ethical considerations relevant for research

There are three levels on which ethical considerations bear on the conduct of research:

- *The official, published standards* are those mandated by the government. They are operative in most universities and other research institutions.
- *Codes of ethics* are those promulgated by professional societies to which researchers belong. For example, the American Anthropological Association (AAA) states that

In both proposing and carrying out our research, anthropological researchers must be open about the purpose(s), potential impacts, and source(s) of support for research projects with funders, colleagues, persons studied or providing information, and with relevant parties affected by the research. Researchers must expect to utilize the results of their work in an appropriate fashion and disseminate the results through appropriate and timely activities. Research fulfilling these expectations is ethical, regardless of the source of funding (public or private) or purpose (i.e., 'applied', 'basic', or 'proprietary').

The AAA goes on to stipulate that the primary responsibility of researchers is to *the people with whom they work and whose lives and cultures they study*; responsibilities to scholarship and the scientific community and to the general public, while important, are secondary to that relationship to the people who provide the substance of the research (see Rynkiewich and Spradley, 1981).

- *Our own personal values* guide us as we attempt to deal fairly and humanely with other people. Personal values may be the product of our religious traditions, the consensus among our peer groups, our own personal reflection on issues of concern, or some combination of all these factors. (See Elliott and Stern, 1997, for a fuller discussion of research ethics.)

Institutional structures

Social research is governed by the structure of institutional review boards (IRBs; see also Flick, 2007b, chap. 9), which since the 1960s have grown out of federal regulations mandating *informed consent* from all those participating in federally funded research. Those participants are, in the regulatory language, referred to as *human subjects*.

The protection of 'human subjects' became an issue as a result of a number of research projects in which experiments (usually of a biomedical or otherwise clinical nature) led to the injury or even death of participants. In order to save subjects from the negative effects of 'intrusive' research procedures, participation in the research was made a *choice* that was under the control of the potential subjects. And in order for them to make a well-reasoned choice, they would have to be informed beforehand about the nature of the project and what, exactly, their participation would entail.

Protecting human research subjects refers not only to saving them from physical or psychological injury. It also refers to safeguarding their privacy and maintaining the confidentiality of all research records that might identify them. Since we cannot always assume we know what potential research subjects do or do not consider matters of privacy that they do not wish anyone outside the research context to know about, we must be very careful in spelling out for them the ways

85

we will keep information from getting out. And we must learn to listen to them when they tell us what is and is not acceptable to them personally or collectively on behalf of their community.

One common procedure is to use codes (numbers or pseudonyms) when describing people in field notes and in any reports generated from the research. The researcher might also want to specify that the notes will be kept in a secure place or that they will be destroyed upon completion of the project. Copies of research records (e.g. tapes and/or transcripts of interviews) could be returned to the subject for approval prior to the publication of any product based on those records.

But unlike members of the clergy, or physicians, or lawyers, ethnographers do not enjoy an automatic privilege of confidentiality. If push comes to shove, our promises to our subjects cannot withstand a court subpoena. Like reporters protecting their sources, we can always opt to refuse to comply with such a subpoena and pay the consequences for that refusal. But not everyone is prepared to follow that high moral ground to its logical conclusions.

The enunciation of a right of informed consent led to the creation of IRBs set up to monitor and enforce compliance at all institutions receiving federal moneys. No researcher would seriously argue *against* that right (or mechanisms to support it), but social scientists have been increasingly concerned about the tendency of IRBs to extend their reach over all forms of research. While the research of social scientists is certainly less likely than biomedical research to have dire physical consequences, it certainly has the potential to harm subjects who have not been properly informed. But in the view of many social scientists, IRBs have been slow to recognize the nuances of difference between 'intrusive' research of the clinical/biomedical sort and of the ethnographic sort.

In the 1980s, the federal government allowed social scientists to claim an exemption from review *unless* they were working with members of designated *vulnerable populations*, including children, people with disabilities, people in prison, and the elderly. Since such people are, for various reasons, less likely to understand the procedures and aims of social research, they are more likely *not* to make a truly informed decision to participate unless extra caution is exercised. In any case, legal counselors at a number of universities (including the one at which this author is based) have advised against IRBs granting this near-blanket exemption. Indeed, at my university, *all* proposals must be reviewed by the IRB, even those that meet the federal criteria for exemption, although they may be deemed eligible for an 'expedited' review. Even proposals that would seem to be unarguably exempt (e.g. studies relying on on-the-record interviews with elected officials about matters of public policy) must still be filed with the IRB. It is ironic that another type of exempt research – that relying on 'unobtrusive' measures, as discussed in an earlier chapter – is the very one about which ethnographic researchers themselves have the most ethical concerns, because the people under study are not supposed to be informed at all that research is going on.

My university now has two IRBs, one for biomedical research and one for 'behavioral research'. The latter, however, is staffed by researchers more familiar with experimental forms of social research than with participant-observer-based ethnography, and they are still not entirely sensitive to the ways in which ethnographic fieldworkers operate. For example, experimental researchers work from strict research protocols, with all questions spelled out in advance and all observational procedures highly structured. While ethnographers may well use similar methods in the field, they also use many methods that cannot be completely explicated beforehand. Things that happen in the course of participant observation cannot always be clearly anticipated, and informal, off-the-cuff interviews are just as common as highly structured ones. These contingencies make it very difficult for ethnographers to produce the sort of research proposal that satisfies the IRBs' understandable desire to have all the possible areas of concern clearly delineated and reviewed before research is authorized.

As a result, even the 'behavioral' research IRB requires a statement of a hypothesis to be tested and a 'protocol for the experiment'. Moreover, of the many hundreds of pages in the federal handbook for IRBs, only eleven paragraphs are devoted to behavioral research. It is now mandated that all principal investigators on IRB-reviewed projects take continuing education on evolving federal ethical standards. It is possible to do so over the Internet, but in the most recent academic year, the choices of training modules were all drawn from the area of health services research. (See Fluehr-Lobban, 2003, for a fuller discussion of ethics and the function of an IRB and also Flick, 2007b, chap. 9)

In a rather surprising recent twist, the Oral History Association has agreed to define what its members do as 'not research' so that they will not have to deal with the IRB at all. Their reasoning is that 'research' is based on experimental design, hypothesis testing, and quantitative analysis. Therefore, oral history (and, by implication, the great bulk of ethnographic research) is not research, but something more akin to what is done in literature and the arts. Ethnographers do not by any means shun affiliation with literature and the arts, but most would reject the notion that what they do is therefore not research. This issue has not been satisfactorily resolved as of this writing. For the time being, then, it is important for all those contemplating ethnographic research to familiarize themselves with the current institutional ethical standards on the assumption that their projects might be entitled to 'expedited' review but are not – and should not be – 'exempt' from review.

The personal dimension of research ethics

Even if an ethnographic researcher has carefully followed the appropriate institutional guidelines for ethical conduct, there are still several situations peculiar to ethnography (particularly that based on participant observation) that raise ethical challenges for the fieldworker.

We must, for example, consider the label now enshrined in federal policy: human *subjects*. The term certainly has clinical and impersonal connotations that are inappropriate to ethnography in general. It also has certain political connotations, reflecting a hierarchical view of the research process. It may once have been the case that the researcher was in control and was in a position to manipulate all the elements in the research design to suit his or her purpose. To a certain extent, this may still be true in the experimental sciences, but it was usually not true of ethnography, and it has become much less true in our own time. Ethnographers are increasingly inclined to think of the people they study as research 'partners' or 'collaborators' rather than as 'subjects'.

Participant observers after all develop their research as they go along. It grows out of the evolving relationship that they cultivate with the people in the study community. In a very important sense, the ethnographic research process is a dialogue between the researcher and the community. While the researcher may have the skills to carry out the data collection and analysis, he or she is almost completely dependent on the cooperation and goodwill of those being studied in order to accomplish that process. Their 'informed consent' must necessarily mean more than that they simply understand what the researcher wants to do 'to' them; they must understand how their own feedback will become part of the plan of what the researcher can do 'with' them.

The research landscape created by the emergence of IRBs heightens the challenge that has always faced ethnographic fieldworkers, namely:

How do you strike an appropriate balance between the intense interactions that are an integral part of the participant observational strategy and the need to maintain some degree of scholarly objectivity so as to be able to present a balanced and persuasive analysis of the community under study?

There is no simple or uniform answer to that question, which is basically a matter of context and situation.

For example, in Trinidad I lived in a family's home and was treated as part of that family unit. My identification with a respected family in the community gave me entrée into the homes and workplaces of others. But it was always very clear that I was not an Indian, not a Trinidadian and, vis-à-vis the AA group, not an alcoholic. I was clearly an outsider in terms of race, ethnicity, educational background, religion, and so forth. I was a sympathetic outsider to be sure, one who was able to establish a warm working relationship with people in the community. But my status as one whose main purpose was to 'write a book' (which is how they understood my scholarly purposes) was never questioned, nor was my need to keep a certain distance so as to see the 'big picture'.

In formal terms, I was no less an outsider to the community of adults with mental retardation, but the men in that group were not always able to distinguish me in my capacity as friend from me in my capacity as someone studying their lives. I could not keep the distance that was recognized and respected in Trinidad with regard to the men in the agency. One of the main reasons, in fact, that I opted to write my book about this project in the form of a fictionalized narrative was because I could not assume the mantle of detached scholarly objectivity that would have been expected in a standard monograph, but that would have been a falsification of the degree to which my friendship with these men had shaped both my analysis and my way of seeing the world in which they lived.

These considerations make it more, rather than less, imperative that ethnographers be mindful of the relational ethics implied by the informed consent process. But human interactions are always situated in some context; it is difficult to squeeze them into universally applicable, objective 'codes' (see Punch, 1986).

Conclusion

An important part of the toolkit of all well-trained ethnographic fieldworkers should be their ability to clearly understand their own values as they bear on respect for others, and to articulate those values in such a way that potential research 'collaborators' can in fact make a reasonably well-informed decision about whether or not they want to participate in a given project.

Key points

- Ethnography involves a close interaction between researchers and those they study. Ethical principles guiding interpersonal relations must therefore be an integral part of the research process for all participant observers/fieldworkers.
- Ethical research decisions are governed by
  - ✓ federal standards monitored and enforced by university institutional review boards
  - ✓ personal values.
- Federal standards are concerned with eliciting informed consent from all human subjects in research and with protecting the privacy of those subjects and the confidentiality of their records.
  - ✓ Ethnographic research, unlike clinical research, *may* be exempt (or receive expedited review) by an IRB unless it deals with a designated vulnerable population.
- On the personal level, there has been a general shift away from thinking of study participants as subjects and toward considering them partners or collaborators in the research process.

Further reading

Ethical considerations are discussed in more detail in the following sources:

Elliott, D. and Stern, J.E. (eds) (1997) *Research Ethics: A Reader*. Hanover, NH: University Press of New England.

Flick, U. (2007b) *Managing Quality in Qualitative Research* (Book 8 of *The SAGE Qualitative Research Kit*). London: Sage.

Fluehr-Lobban, C. (ed.) (2003) *Ethics and the Profession of Anthropology: Dialogue for Ethically Conscious Practice* (2nd ed.). Walnut Creek, CA: AltaMira.

Punch, M. (1986) *The Politics and Ethics of Fieldwork*. Beverly Hills, CA: Sage.

Rynkiewich, M.A. and Spradley, J.P. (1981) *Ethics and Anthropology: Dilemmas in Fieldwork*. Malabar, FL: Krieger.

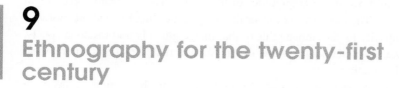

9
Ethnography for the twenty-first century

Chapter objectives
After reading this chapter you should know more about

- the ways in which the conduct of participant observation and fieldwork has changed; and
- how this is a consequence of changing circumstances in both the 'real' and the 'virtual' world of modern technology, communication, and transportation.

Most of the data collection tools discussed in this volume were developed more than a hundred years ago for research in small-scale, homogeneous, traditional societies. They are still most definitely useful and important parts of our contemporary tool-kits. But the contexts in which we use them have changed radically.

The changing research context: technology

Participant observation once implied a lone researcher working in a self-contained community, armed only with a notebook and pen, and perhaps a sketch pad and a simple camera. The mechanics of research were revitalized by the introduction of audiotape recorders, movie cameras, and later video recorders. Note-taking has been transformed by the advent of laptop computers and software programs for the analysis of narrative data.

But as our technological sophistication increases, ethnographers have begun to realize that the technology helps us capture and fix 'reality' in ways that are somewhat at variance with our lived experience as fieldworkers. The great value of participant observation research has been that we have immersed ourselves in the ebb and flow, in the ambiguities of life as it is lived by real people in real circumstances. The more we fix this or that snapshot of that life and the more we have the capacity to disseminate this or that image globally and instantaneously, the more we risk violating our sense of what makes real life so particular and so endlessly fascinating.

Perhaps it will become necessary for us to turn our observational powers on the very process of observation, to understand ourselves as users of technology. Technological change is never merely additive, that is, never simply an aid to doing what has always been done. It is, rather, *ecological* in the sense that a change in one aspect of behavior has ramifications throughout the entire system of which that behavior is a part. So the more sophisticated our technology, the more we change the way we do business. We need to begin to understand not only what happens when 'we' encounter 'them', but when 'we' do so with a particular kind of powerful technology. (See Nardi and O'Day, 1999, for an elaboration of these points.)

The changing research context: globalization

Globalization is the process by which capital, goods, services, labor, ideas, and other cultural forms move freely across international borders. In our own time, communities that once existed in some degree of isolation have been drawn into interdependent relationships that extend around the globe.

Globalization has been facilitated by the growth of information technology. News from all corners of the world is instantaneously available. While once we could assume that the behaviors and ideas we observed or asked about in a particular community were somehow indigenous to that community, now we must ask literally where in the world they might have come from.

Communities are no longer necessarily place-bound, and the traditional influences of geography, topography, climate, and so forth are much less fixed than in days past. Many Trinidadians, for example, are now *transnational*, including members of the once defiantly insular Indian community. Even in fairly recent times people would migrate to England or Canada or the United States for education or job opportunities; but once they went, they usually stayed. Nowadays they can and do go back and forth, often maintaining homes both on the island and 'away'. Being an 'Indian' once had a definite meaning within the context of the small island. What does it mean now when one is shuttling between the West Indies and some other place? In New York or London or Toronto, is that person an 'Indian', a 'Trinidadian', a 'West Indian', or some combination of factors? A generation ago that question would have made no sense to the people I began studying in the early 1970s. But now the 'community' exists all over the place and its identity is by no means as neatly fixed as people thirty years ago would have thought.

Doing participant observation in a 'transnational' community presents obvious challenges. We could, of course, contrive to follow people around the globe, but that hardly seems practical in most cases. More often than not, we will continue to be place-bound researchers, but we will have to keep reminding ourselves that the 'place' we are participating in and observing may no longer be the total social or cultural reality for all the people who are in some way or another affiliated with that community.

We can discern several aspects of the modern world that may help us take ethnographic methods such as observation beyond their origins in small-scale traditional communities:

- Analysts now speak of the emergence of a *world system*, a world in which nations are economically and politically interdependent. The world system and the relations among the units within that system are shaped in large measure by the global capitalist economy, which is committed to the maximization of profits rather than to the satisfaction of domestic needs. Some settings and events that might be studied by the methods discussed in this volume so as to contribute to our understanding of the world system are:
    - ✓ the nature of labor migration (see, e.g., Zúñiga and Hernández-León, 2001, who describe the ways in which Latino laborers coming to the United States have been shifting out of agriculture and into the industrial sector);
    - ✓ the emergence of 'outsourcing' and its impact on the traditional societies that are thus brought into the world of the dominant powers (see, e.g., Saltzinger, 2003, a study of Mexican factory workers).

- The transformation of what was once the Soviet sphere of influence has led to many social as well as economic and political changes. One scholar who has begun to document them is Janine Wedel (2002).
- The world has always been culturally diverse, of course. But now that globalization is bringing different cultures into more frequent contact with each other, the dynamic of cultural diversity, multiculturalism, and culture contact is shifting dramatically. (See, e.g., Maybury-Lewis, 2002, a study of indigenous peoples and ethnicity in the contemporary world.)
- In the modern world, people are less defined by traditions of 'high culture'. They are more likely to be influenced (and to be drawn together as a global 'community') by popular culture. The study of popular culture has been a staple of 'cultural studies' for some time, and it is now well established in the mainstream disciplines as well. (See, e.g., Bird, 2003; Fiske, 1989; Fiske and Hartley, 2003; see also Ong and Collier, 2005, for an extended treatment

of the implications of globalization on social research in general, and ethnographic research in particular.)

The changing research context: virtual worlds

If they so choose, ethnographers can free themselves of 'place' by means of the Internet. *Virtual communities* are now common; they are characterized not by geographic proximity or long-established ties of heritage, but by computer-mediated communication and online interactions. They are 'communities of interest' rather than communities of residence. While some can last a while, they are mostly ephemeral in nature – they come and go as participants' interests change.

Ethnography can certainly be carried out online. One can 'observe' the goings-on in an Internet chat room in much the same way that one could observe the doings in a traditional 'place'. One can conduct interviews over the Internet. And our ability to use archival materials have clearly been improved by methods of digital storage and retrieval. Living online is becoming a twenty-first-century commonplace, and ethnography can certainly move into cyberspace along with the technology.

Some cautions, however, are in order:

- Electronic communication is based almost exclusively on the written word, or on deliberately chosen images. The ethnographer who is used to 'reading' behavior through the nuances of gesture, facial expression, and tone of voice is therefore at something of a disadvantage.
- It is very easy for people online to disguise their identities – sometimes the whole purpose of participating in an online group is to assume a whole new identity.
- If you are doing the kind of research that depends on the 'accuracy' of 'facts', then it will be necessary to develop a critical sense, to evaluate virtual sources carefully, and to avoid making claims of certainty that cannot be backed up by other means.

But are 'virtual communities' really all that similar to traditional communities or social networks? How does electronic communication bring new communities into existence even as it enhances the way older, established communities, now geographically dispersed, can keep in touch? Such questions lead us to the possibilities of research not only about specific people and their lives, but also about the larger processes by which people define their lives.

Virtual ethnography also poses some ethical challenges that are similar to – but not exactly the same as – those that confront the fieldworker in traditional communities. It goes without saying that the accepted norms of informed consent and protection of privacy and confidentiality continue to be important, even though we are dealing with people we do not see face-to-face. While the Internet is a kind of public space, the people who 'inhabit' it are still individuals entitled to the same rights as people in more conventional 'places'. There are as yet no comprehensive ethical guidelines applicable to online research, but a few principles seem to be emerging by consensus:

- Research based on a content analysis of a public website need not pose an ethical problem and it is *probably* acceptable to quote messages posted on public message boards, as long as the quotes are not attributed to identifiable correspondents.
- Members of an online community should be informed if an ethnographer is also online 'observing' their activities for research purposes.
- Members of a virtual community under observation should be assured that the researcher will not use real names, e-mail addresses, or any other identifying markers in any publication based on the research.
- If the online group has posted its rules for entering and participating, those norms should be honored by the researcher, just as he or she would respect the values and expectations of any other community in which he or she intended to act as a participant observer.

Some online ethnographers have also adopted the practice of sharing drafts of research reports for comment by members of the virtual community. By allowing members to help decide how their comments are to be used, the researcher thereby accomplishes the larger ethical goal of turning 'subjects' into truly empowered 'collaborators'.

The anthropologist David Hakken (2003) has been conducting a long-term study of the computer revolution; he has created what he terms an 'ethnography of computing'. He notes that most of the rapidly proliferating computer systems were designed and implemented in a 'machine-centered' manner. However, real computing takes place in highly social organizations (businesses, schools, governments) where the exclusive focus on the machine (and the code for operating the machine) was incompatible with the culture of the users. There is a movement toward a more 'human-centered' approach to the design of computing systems, but Hakken notes that even such user-friendly developments are individualistic in nature and do not sufficiently reflect the social nature of computing. He therefore proposes what he calls a 'culture-centered' computing model. Thinking culturally about new technology would allow for the building of effective systems and for raising the broader ethical and political issues posed by revolutionary technology. It would also emphasize the implications of such technologies on the practices of the various academic disciplines that now increasingly rely on computers to conduct their activities. Because researchers dealing with cyberspace are working with social formations that are as much potential as existing in current real time (that is, they are perpetually 'under construction'), an ethical posture that is 'active' and anticipatory is needed, in contrast to the essentially reactive ethics of

95

prior forms of research. The dimensions of such an ethical program have not, however, been completely worked out, let alone widely adopted by researchers in the various social sciences. (See Hine, 2000; Jones 1999; Markham, 1996; and Miller and Slater, 2000, for further discussion of the challenges of virtual research.)

Key points

- Ethnographic data collection tools designed for use in small-scale, homogeneous, traditional societies are still useful, but we must be aware of changes in the context of research.
- The technology available to the modern ethnographer enhances his or her ability to do fieldwork, but also runs the risk of 'fixing' the moment with such clarity and apparent finality that the flux of real life is no longer captured.
- The process of globalization by which capital, goods, services, labor, ideas, and other cultural forms move across international boundaries has created transnational communities in which social relations are no longer place-bound. Studying social structure, cultural values, and group identities must now be undertaken in a wider arena.
- It is possible to use traditional ethnographic methods of observation, interviewing, and archival research in the virtual communities online, but we stand in need of research on the actual nature of those communities. Greater attention must also be paid to the extension of ethical guidelines from the study of traditional communities to virtual ones.

Further reading

The following authors discuss the issues mentioned in this chapter in more detail:

Hakken, D. (2003) 'An ethics for an anthropology in and of cyberspace', in C. Fluehr-Lobban (ed.), *Ethics and the Profession of Anthropology: Dialogue for Ethically Conscious Practice* (2nd ed.). Walnut Creek, CA: AltaMira, pp. 179–95.

Miller, D. and Slater D. (2000) *The Internet: An Ethnographic Approach*. New York: Berg.

Ong, A. and Collier S.J. (2005) *Global Assemblages: Technology, Politics, and Ethics as Anthropological Problems*. Malden, MA: Blackwell.

III Glossary

Applied ethnography The use of ethnographic research methods so that findings can make a contribution to the formulation and maintenance of policies or procedures that serve the community under study.

Archival research The analysis of records and other materials that have been stored for research, service, and other purposes both official and unofficial.

Behavior trace studies The use of artifacts left behind by people as a way of understanding their behaviors.

Critical theory A general term covering a variety of approaches to the study of contemporary society and culture; the linking theme is the use of social science to challenge the assumptions of the dominant institutions of society.

Cultural studies A field of research particularly concerned with institutions such as the mass media and popular culture that represent convergences of history, ideology, and subjective experience.

Culture The shared, learned beliefs, material products, and social actions that characterize a social group.

Descriptive analysis The process of breaking data down into its component parts so as to discern patterns or regularities in those data.

Emic analysis A way of understanding a study community by focusing on the way people in that community give meaning to their actions.

Ethnocentrism The tendency to think that one's own culture represents the best or most logical way to understand and act in the world.

Ethnographic survey A closed-ended research instrument designed to collect quantitative data from a relatively large number of informants.

Ethnography A descriptive study of a group of people.

Ethnomethodology An approach to social research that focuses on how a social group's sense of reality is constructed, maintained, and changed, rather than on the specific content of that sense of reality.

Etic analysis A way of understanding a study community by discerning the ways its behaviors match up with patterns that appear to be cross-culturally valid.

Feminism An approach to social research that focuses on the centrality of gender as a determinant of the social order.

Field work Social research conducted in the natural settings where people live or work.

Gatekeepers Members of a potential study community who control a researcher's access to that community.

Genealogical interview A method of collecting systematic information about kinship and related social networks.

Hierarchical tree A diagram showing different levels of abstraction in the interpretation of some social or cultural phenomenon.

Inductive inquiry The use of accumulated empirical evidence to build toward a general explanatory theory.

Informed consent A basic principle of research ethics; people are expected to agree to participate in a research project after they have been given all the pertinent information about the methods and projected outcomes of the research.

Interviewing A process of directing a conversation in a systematic way so as to collect information.

Kinesics The study of 'body language'.

Life history A type of interview that reconstructs the life of a person, who is construed as *either* a representative member of a particular social group *or* an exemplar of that group's ideals or aspirations.

Marxism A theory that links economics, politics, and history by positing inequalities of socioeconomic class as the determining factor of the social order, and by upholding the necessity of class conflict as the driving force of historical change.

Matrix A table allowing for the comparison of two or more segments of a population in terms of a designated factor in the perceived behavior of the community.

Observation A tool of social inquiry in which the activities and relationships of people in the study community are perceived through the five senses of the researcher.

Oral history A field of study dedicated to the reconstruction of the past through the personal recollections of those who have lived it.

Participant observation A way of conducting ethnographic research that places the researcher in the midst of, and interacting with, the community under study.

Postmodernism A movement in the social sciences that challenges the assumption that the study of society and culture should emulate the objective scientific method.

Proposition A research question that states an association between presumed variables but does not use the format of a formal, testable hypothesis.

Proxemics The study of the ways in which space is arranged so as to convey social meanings.

Reliability A measure of the degree to which any given observation is consistent with a general pattern and not the result of random chance.

Representations The ways in which ethnographic data are conveyed to the public.

Semi-structured interview The use of predetermined questions related to domains of interest in the study community.

Structure-functionalism A theory that treats society as a balanced, relatively static collectivity of institutions.

Symbolic interactionism A theory that treats social life as a product of ongoing and ever-changing encounters among members of the community.

Theoretical analysis The process of explaining patterns or regularities that appear in the descriptive analysis of data.

Thick description The presentation of details, context, emotions, and the nuances of social relationships in order to evoke the 'feeling' of a scene and not just its surface attributes.

Triangulation The use of multiple data sources to verify the findings of social research.

Unobtrusive observation The use of research techniques in such a way that those under study do not know that they are being observed.

Validity A measure of the degree to which a research finding actually demonstrates what it appears to demonstrate.

Verisimilitude A style of writing that draws the reader into the world that has been studied so as to evoke a mood of recognition.

Virtual communities Groups defined by computer-mediated communication and online interactions rather than by geographic proximity.

Vulnerable populations Groups, such as children, people with disabilities, prisoners, and the elderly, who are considered to be at special risk of exploitation, and whose rights as research subjects must be especially safeguarded.

III References

This list includes the references quoted in the book and some additional but helpful references about the field of doing ethnographic research.

Adler, P.A. and Adler, P. (1994) 'Observational techniques', in N.K. Denzin and Y.S. Lincoln (eds), *Handbook of Qualitative Research* (1st ed.). Thousand Oaks, CA: Sage, pp. 377–92 (2nd ed. 2000).

Agar, M. (1980) *The Professional Stranger: An Informal Introduction to Ethnography.* San Diego: Academic Press.

Agar, M.H. (1986) *Speaking of Ethnography.* Beverly Hills, CA: Sage.

Anderson, E. (1990). *Streetwise.* Chicago: University of Chicago Press.

Angrosino, M.V. (1974) *Outside is Death: Alcoholism, Ideology, and Community Organization among the East Indians in Trinidad.* Winson-Salem, NC: Medical Behavioral Science Monograph Series.

Angrosino, M.V. (1998) *Opportunity House: Ethnographic Stories of Mental Retardation.* Walnut Creek, CA: AltaMira.

Angrosino, M.V. (ed.) (2002) *Doing Cultural Anthropology: Projects for Ethnographic Data Collection.* Prospect Heights, IL: Waveland.

Angrosino, M.V. and A. Mays de Pérez, K. (2000) 'Rethinking observation: from method to context', in N.K. Denzin and Y.S. Lincoln (eds), *Handbook of Qualitative Research* (2nd ed.). Thousand Oaks, CA: Sage, pp. 673–702

Atkinson, P., Coffey, A., Delamont, S., Lofland, J. and Lofland, L. (eds) (2001) *Handbook of Ethnography.* London: Sage.

Babbie, E. (1986) *Observing Ourselves: Essays in Social Research.* Prospect Heights, IL: Waveland.

Banks, M. (2007) *Using Visual Data in Qualitative Research* (Book 5 of *The SAGE Qualitative Research Kit*). London: Sage.

Banks, A. and Stephen, P. (eds) (1998) *Fiction and Social Research: By Ice or Fire.* Walnut Creek, CA: AltaMira.

Barbour, R. (2007) *Doing Focus Groups* (Book 4 of *The SAGE Qualitative Research Kit*). London: Sage.

Berg, B.L. (2004) *Qualitative Research Methods for the Social Sciences,* (5th ed.). Boston: Pearson.

Bernard, H.R. (1988) *Research Methods in Cultural Anthropology.* Newbury Park, CA: Sage.

Bird, S.E. (2003). *The Audience in Everyday Life: Living in a Media World.* New York: Routledge.

Bochner, A.P. and Ellis, C. (2002) *Ethnographically Speaking: Autoethnography, Literature, and Aesthetics.* Walnut Creek, CA: AltaMira.

Bogdan, R.C. and Biklen, S.K. (2003) *Qualitative Research for Education: An Introduction to Theory and Methods* (4th ed.). Boston: Allyn & Bacon.

Borzak, L. (ed.) (1981) *Field Study: A Sourcebook for Experiential Learning*. Beverly Hills, CA: Sage.

Bourgois, P. (1995) 'Workaday world, crack economy', *The Nation*, 261: 706–11.

Cahill, S.E. (1985) 'Meanwhile backstage: public bathrooms and the interaction order', *Urban Life*, 14: 33–58.

Chambers, E. (2000) 'Applied ethnography', in N.K. Denzin and Y.S. Lincoln (eds), *Handbook of Qualitative Research* (2nd ed.). Thousand Oaks, CA: Sage, pp. 851–69.

Clifford, J. and Marcus, G. (eds) (1986) *Writing Culture: The Poetics and Politics of Ethnography*. Berkeley: University of California Press.

Crane, J.G. and Angrosino, M.V. (1992) *Field Projects in Anthropology: A Student Handbook* (3rd ed.). Prospect Heights, IL: Waveland.

Creswell, J.W. (1994) *Research Design: Qualitative and Quantitative Approaches*. Thousand Oaks, CA: Sage.

Creswell, J.W. (1998) *Qualitative Inquiry and Research Design: Choosing among Five Traditions*. Thousand Oaks, CA: Sage.

de Matta, R. (1994) 'Some biased remarks on interpretism', in R. Borofsky (ed.), *Assessing Cultural Anthropology*. New York: McGraw-Hill, pp. 119–32.

Denzin, N.K. and Lincoln, Y.S. (eds) (2003) *Collecting and Interpreting Qualitative Materials* (2nd ed.). Thousand Oaks, CA: Sage.

DeVita, P.R. (1992) *The Naked Anthropologist: Tales from around the World*. Belmont, CA: Wadsworth.

Elliott, D. and Stern, J.E. (eds) (1997) *Research Ethics: A Reader*. Hanover, NH: University Press of New England.

Ellis, C. (1995) *Final Negotiations: A Story of Love, Loss, and Chronic Illness*. Philadelphia: Temple University Press.

Ellis, C. and Bochner, A.P. (eds) (1996) *Composing Ethnography: Alternative Forms of Qualitative Writing*. Walnut Creek, CA: AltaMira.

Emerson, R.M. (ed.) (2001) *Contemporary Field Research* (2nd ed.). Prospect Heights, IL: Waveland.

Erikson, K.T. (1967) 'A comment on disguised observation in sociology', *Social Problems*, 14: 366–73.

Fetterman, D.M. (1998) *Ethnography Step by Step* (2nd ed.). Thousand Oaks, CA: Sage.

Fiske, J. (1989) *Understanding Popular Culture*. Boston: Unwin Hyman.

Fiske, J. and Hartley, J. (2003) *Reading Television* (2nd ed.). New York: Routledge.

Flick, U. (2006) *An Introduction to Qualitative Research* (3rd ed.). London: Sage.

Flick, U. (2007a) *Designing Qualitative Research* (Book 1 of *The SAGE Qualitative Research Kit*). London: Sage.

Flick, U. (2007b) *Managing Quality in Qualitative Research* (Book 8 of *The SAGE Qualitative Research Kit*). London: Sage.

Flick, U., Kardorff, E. von and Steinke, I. (eds) (2004) *A Companion to Qualitative Research* (trans. B. Jenner). London: Sage.

Fluehr-Lobban, C. (ed.) (2003) *Ethics and the Profession of Anthropology: Dialogue for Ethically Conscious Practice* (2nd ed.). Walnut Creek, CA: AltaMira.

Fox, K.J. (2001) 'Self-change and resistance in prison', in J.A. Halberstein and J.F. Gubrium (eds), *Institutional Selves: Troubled Identities in the Postmodern World*. New York: Oxford University Press, pp. 176–92.

Geertz, C. (1973) 'Thick description: toward an interpretive theory of culture', in C. Geertz, *The Interpretation of Cultures*. New York: Basic Books, pp. 3–30.

Gibbs, G.R. (2007) *Analyzing Qualitative Data.* (Book 6 of *The SAGE Qualitative Research Kit*). London: Sage.

Goffman, E. (1971) *Relations in Public.* New York: Basic Books.

Gold, R.L. (1958) 'Roles in sociological field observations', *Social Forces,* 36: 217–23.

Guba, E.G. and. Lincoln Y.S. (2005) 'Paradigmatic controversies, contradictions, and emerging confluences', in N.K. Denzin and Y.S. Lincoln (eds), *Handbook of Qualitative Research,* (3rd ed.). Thousand Oaks, CA: Sage, pp. 191–215.

Hakken, D. (2003) 'An ethics for an anthropology in and of cyberspace', in C. Fluehr-Lobban (ed.), *Ethics and the Profession of Anthropology: Dialogue for Ethically Conscious Practice* (2nd ed.). Walnut Creek, CA: AltaMira, pp. 179–95.

Heider, K. (1976) *Ethnographic Film.* Austin: University of Texas Press.

Herman, N.J. and Reynolds, L.T. (1994) *Symbolic Interaction: An Introduction to Social Psychology.* Dix Hills, NY: General Hall.

Hine, C. (2000) *Virtual Ethnography.* London: Sage.

Humphreys, L. (1975) *Tearoom Trade: Impersonal Sex in Public Places.* New York: Aldine.

Janesick, V.J. (1998) *'Stretching' Exercises for Qualitative Researchers.* Thousand Oaks, CA: Sage.

Jones, S.G. (ed.) (1999) *Doing Internet Research: Critical Issues and Methods for Examining the Net.* London: Sage.

Kvale, S. (2007) *Doing Interviews* (Book 2 of *The SAGE Qualitative Research Kit*). London: Sage.

LeCompte, M.D. and Schensul, J.J. (1999) *Designing and Conducting Ethnographic Research* (Vol. I of J.J. Schensul, S.L. Schensul and M.D. LeCompte, (eds), *Ethnographer's Toolkit*). Walnut Creek, CA: AltaMira.

McGee, R.J. and Warms, R.L. (2003) *Anthropological Theory: An Introductory History,* (3rd ed.). Boston: McGraw-Hill.

Malinowski, B. (1922) *Argonauts of the Western Pacific.* London: Routledge.

Marcus, G. (ed.) (1999) *Critical Anthropology Now: Unexpected Contexts, Shifting Constituencies, Changing Agendas.* Santa Fe, NM: School of American Research Press.

Marcus, G. and Fischer, M. (1986) *Anthropology as Cultural Critique: An Experimental Moment in the Human Sciences.* Chicago: University of Chicago Press.

Markham, A. (1996) *Life On-Line: Researching Real Experience in Virtual Space.* Walnut Creek, CA: AltaMira.

Mason, J. (2002). *Qualitative Researching* (2nd ed.). London: Sage.

Maybury-Lewis, D. (2002) *Indigenous People, Ethnic Groups, and the State* (2nd ed.). Boston: Allyn & Bacon.

Mehan, H. and Wood, H. (1975) *The Reality of Ethnomethodology.* New York: Wiley.

Mienczakowski, J. (1996) 'The ethnographic act', in C. Ellis and A. Bochner (eds), *Composing Ethnography: Alternative Forms of Qualitative Writing.* Walnut Creek, CA: AltaMira, pp. 244–64.

Miles, M.B. and Huberman, A.M. (1994) *Qualitative Data Analysis: An Expanded Sourcebook* (2nd ed.). Thousand Oaks, CA: Sage.

Miller, D. and Slater, D. (2000). *The Internet: An Ethnographic Approach.* New York: Berg.

Morgen, S. (1989) *Gender and Anthropology: Critical Reviews for Research and Teaching.* Washington, DC: American Anthropological Association.

Nanda, S. (2002) 'Using a museum as a resource for ethnographic research', in M. Angrosino (ed.), *Doing Cultural Anthropology: Projects for Ethnographic Data Collection.* Prospect Heights, IL: Waveland, pp. 71–80.

Nardi, B. and O'Day, V. (1999) *Information Ecologies: Using Technology with Heart.* Cambridge, MA: MIT Press.

Ong, A. and Collier, S.J. (2005) *Global Assemblages: Technology, Politics, and Ethics as Anthropological Problems*. Malden, MA: Blackwell.

Plummer, K. (2005) 'Critical humanism and queer theory: living with the tensions', in N.K. Denzin and Y.S. Lincoln (eds), *Handbook of Qualitative Research*. Thousand Oaks, CA: Sage, pp. 357–74.

Punch, M. (1986) *The Politics and Ethics of Fieldwork*. Beverly Hills, CA: Sage.

Rapley, T. (2007) *Doing Conversation, Discourse and Document Analysis* (Book 7 of *The SAGE Qualitative Research Kit*). London: Sage.

Richardson, L. (1990) *Writing Strategies: Reaching Diverse Audiences*. Newbury Park, CA: Sage.

Richardson, L. (1992) 'The consequences of poetic representation', in C. Ellis and M. Flaherty (eds), *Investigating Subjectivity*. London: Sage, pp. 125–40.

Rossman, G.B. and Rallis, S.F. (1998) *Learning in the Field: An Introduction to Qualitative Research*. Thousand Oaks, CA: Sage.

Rynkiewich, M.A. and Spradley, J.P. (1981) *Ethics and Anthropology: Dilemmas in Fieldwork*. Malabar, FL: Krieger.

Saltzinger, L. (2003) *Genders in Production: Making Workers in Mexico's Global Factories*. Berkeley: University of California Press.

Schensul, J.J. (1999) 'Building community research partnerships in the struggle against AIDS', *Health Education and Behaviour*, 26 (special issue).

Schensul, S.L., Schensul, J.J. and LeCompte, M.D. (1999) *Essential Ethnographic Methods: Observations, Interviews, and Questionnaires* (Vol. II of J.J. Schensul, S.L Schensul and M., LeCompte, (eds), *Ethnographer's Toolkit*). Walnut Creek, CA: AltaMira.

Scrimshaw, S.C. and Gleason, G.R. (eds) (1992) *RAP: Rapid Assessment Procedures: Qualitative Methodologies for Planning and Evaluation of Health-Related Programs*. Boston: International Nutritional Foundation for Developing Countries.

Seale, C. (1999) *The Quality of Qualitative Research*. London: Sage.

Seale, C., Gobo, G., Gubrium, J. and Silverman, D. (eds) (2004) *Qualitative Research Practice*. London: Sage.

Sparkes, A.C. (2002) *Telling Tales in Sport and Physical Activity: A Qualitative Journey*. Champaign, IL: Human Kinetics.

Spradley, J.P. (1980) *Participant Observation*. New York: Holt, Rinehart & Winston.

Storey, J. (1998) *An Introduction to Cultural Theory and Popular Culture* (2nd ed.). Athens: University of Georgia Press.

Toumey, C.P. (1994) *God's Own Scientists: Creationists in a Secular World*. New Brunswick, NJ: Rutgers University Press.

Turner, J.H. (1978) *The Structure of Sociological Theory*. Homewood, IL: Dorsey.

van Maanen, J. (ed.) (1982) *Qualitative Methodology*. Beverly Hills, CA: Sage.

van Maanen, J. (1988) *Tales of the Field: On Writing Ethnography*. Chicago: University of Chicago Press.

Wedel, J. (2002) *Blurring the Boundaries of the State-Private Divide: Implications for Corruption*, http://www.anthrobase.com/Txt/W/Wedel_J-01.htm.

Weitzman, E.A. and Miles, M.B. (1995) *Computer Programs for Qualitative Data Analysis*. Thousand Oaks, CA: Sage.

Wiseman, J.P. and Aron, M.S. (1970) *Field Projects for Sociology Students*. Cambridge, MA: Schenkman.

Wolcott, H.F. (1994) 'The elementary school principal: notes from a field study', in H.F. Wolcott (ed.), *Transforming Qualitative Data*. Thousand Oaks, CA: Sage, pp. 103–48.

Wolf, E.R. (1982) *Europe and the People without History*. Berkeley: University of California Press.

Zinn, M.B. (1979) 'Insider field research in minority communities', *Social Problems*, 27: 209–19.

Zúñiga, V. and Hernández-León, R. (2001) 'A new destination for an old migration: origins, trajectories, and labor market incorporation of Latinos in Dalton, Georgia', in A.D. Murphy, C. Blanchard and J.A. Hill (eds), *Latino Workers in the Contemporary South*. Athens: University of Georgia Press, pp. 126–46

▌▌▌ Author index

▌▌▌ Subject index